Revealed preference of government

Revealed preference of government

KAUSHIK BASU

Delhi School of Economics

CAMBRIDGE UNIVERSITY PRESS

CAMBRIDGE

LONDON   NEW YORK   NEW ROCHELLE
MELBOURNE   SYDNEY

Published by the Press Syndicate of the University of Cambridge
The Pitt Building, Trumpington Street, Cambridge CB2 1RP
32 East 57th Street, New York, NY 10022, USA
296 Beaconsfield Parade, Middle Park, Melbourne 3206, Australia

First published 1980

Printed in Great Britain at the University Press, Cambridge

Library of Congress Cataloguing in Publication Data
Basu, Kaushik.
Revealed preference of government.
A revision of the author's thesis, University of
London.
Bibliography: p.
Includes indexes.
1.   Welfare economics — Mathematical models.   I.   Title.
HB99.3.B34   1979   330.15'5   78-67300
ISBN 0 521 22489 6

To my parents

Contents

Preface

Governments, like 'individual guinea-pigs', allegedly reveal their preference by their choices. This belief underlies large areas of economics and has been used explicitly to evaluate government preferences. The present book is an analytical critique of such attempts. Studies of this kind are necessarily interdisciplinary and, consequently, I draw upon theoretical tools from many areas of the social sciences, particularly welfare economics. I have tried to elucidate some of the more abstruse results of welfare economics and to bring them to bear upon practical issues.

This book is a revised version of my PhD dissertation submitted to the University of London. Most of the ideas have germinated during my years as a graduate and a research student at the London School of Economics. I owe a special debt to LSE for having provided a particularly stimulating atmosphere. Since then, I have been at the University of Reading and at the Delhi School of Economics, where I have met and discussed with many interesting economists, some of whom will probably never emerge from obscurity because of an aversion to writing.

In the process of revising my thesis I have attempted to tie up the more mathematical analyses into compact sections. A reader wishing to avoid technicalities may skip the starred sections and appendices. Moreover, I have attempted to make most chapters self-contained as far as possible. The first two chapters are, however, essential reading for proceeding further.

My biggest debt is to my supervisor, Professor Amartya Sen. Not only did he make relevant criticisms on the text, I also had many discussions with him which provided the enthusiasm so essential for research. Around late 1976, the Research Workshop at LSE was revived at the initiative of Max Steuer and some PhD students. I presented two papers to this workshop and faced unusually receptive audiences. I also benefited from comments on papers presented to the University of Reading and University of Kent staff seminars. In appreciation of the many useful suggestions made to me, I should mention Richard Goodwin, K. G. Binmore, Kotaro Suzumura, Charles Sutcliffe, David de Meza, Gautam Sen, Bhaskar Datta and the referees of Cambridge University Press.

For informal discussions, often prolonged, I am grateful to my wife Alaka. I should also record my appreciation of Kulbir Singh's useful secretarial assistance. Finally, I would like to thank the various typists who have assisted me and also encouraged me by their charges to keep the book brief and precise.

Delhi School of Economics   K. C. BASU

1

Introduction

Introduction

An act of choice usually involves both factual information and subjective preference. A government or any decision-making agent, once armed with information regarding the characteristics of a group of projects, can use its preference to choose an 'optimal project'. Considerable attention has been paid to such optimisation processes in economic theory. But consider the opposite problem: A government is observed to choose one project from an available set. Is it possible to infer the implicit preference pattern which guides the government? The few who have tried to solve this problem have come out with conflicting answers. Clearly, the precise preference of the government cannot, in general, be deduced by observing a *single* choice, because there will usually be a whole set of preference patterns which could make the chosen project optimal. But it has been alleged that if we observe many choices, we can narrow down the possible preference patterns and may even be able to reveal the exact one. This issue forms the central theme of our discussions.

Revealed preference analysis calls for a closer scrutiny of the concept of governmental rationality. The assumption of a 'rational' government is embedded in many areas of economics. In what sense and under what conditions can a government be thought of as a rational agent? This question is of wide interest. It raises many issues which are discussed through the book.

Our analysis begins on familiar grounds. Some standard approaches to revealed preference (Weisbrod, 1968; UNIDO, 1972) are formalised in a simple model in the next chapter. It is assumed that social welfare, as conceived by the government, depends on certain observable characteristics of the economy, and each project is a bundle of characteristics. The model is based on the assumption that the project chosen by the government generates at least as much welfare as any project which, in spite of being 'feasible', is rejected. This is a strong assumption. It requires governments to have knife-edged rationality. Weakening this assumption forms the basis of our generalised model in Chapter 3. This model permits the government to have less than perfect precision. Informally speaking, this means that the government can for instance, instead of regarding one unit of unemployment to be worth exactly three units of inflation, think of it as being somewhere between two and four units.

What causes the kind of quasi-determinateness which our generalised model is capable of handling? Quite a few answers to this are given in the book; and a particularly interesting one is related to the problem of interpersonal comparisons. While the individual consumer, in choosing between different combinations of commodities, has very little to do with interpersonal comparisons, this problem looms large in governmental decision-making, since conflicts of interest are frequently involved here. What happens if a government lacks the ability to fully compare interpersonal welfares? According to the traditional theory, which treats interpersonal comparisons as a 0–1 concept, this would imply a *total* inability to compare utilities on the part of the government. This is unrealistic and fortunately we need not accept this position. The concept of 'partial comparison' developed by Sen (1970, 1970a) allows for the possibility that one has only 'rough' notions regarding interpersonal utilities. Though this concept has been discussed by many since its inception, most of the literature is abstruse and mathematical. Chapter 6 contains a simple exposition of partial interpersonal comparisons. Now if a government could only partially compare utilities, then, not surprisingly, this vagueness would be transmitted to the government's preferences over projects. The sort of quasi-determinateness in preference caused by this is the kind which the generalised model is designed to handle.

Other causes of lack of precision are discussed in Chapter 3. It has been argued by Armstrong (1939) that human perceptions are blurred, and it is possible that while an individual is 'indifferent' between n and $n + 1$ granules of sugar in his tea, for all values of n, he prefers two spoons of sugar to none. This casts doubts on the transitivity of indifference and causes some indeterminateness in choice.

While the generalised model accommodates a larger range of behaviour, it has the shortcoming of revealing the government preference less 'closely' than the standard model. The standard approach and, consequently, the Weisbrod and UNIDO models are demonstrated to be a special case of the generalised model. To state the obvious, there will be many situations, some of which are discussed here, where even the generalised model will be unsuitable for analysing behaviour. After all, in studying the revealed preference of Samuelson's 'individual guinea-pigs' one confronts many fundamental problems; and when it comes to analysing governmental behaviour, it is natural that the complexities are much more serious.

Most models of revealed preference are based on the assumption that a government, facing a choice among feasible projects, chooses one which gives maximum welfare. This assumption is supposed to be a logical consequence of the more fundamental assumption that governments maximise welfare. The existence of evaluation costs of projects snaps this logical arrow, so that even if the latter assumption is granted, the former may not hold. What is more intriguing, the existence of evaluation costs may even jeopardise the latter assumption. If evaluation is thought of as an activity, then whether to evaluate or not is itself a choice which the government has to make and this choice may in turn have its own evaluation cost. It is obvious that we are at the threshold of an infinite chain. This is discussed in Chapter 5. The importance of this issue depends on how likely it is that choice involves costly evaluation. Government projects are complex and their evaluation is invariably expensive, since planners have to be employed and information has to be gathered. While the choices of *individuals* do not usually necessitate overt expenditures, they often require at least thought. And, as Ogden Nash observes, even 'thought requires the time and effort to reflect, cogitate, contemplate, meditate, ruminate and ponder'.[1] There are, however, many situations in which, being familiar with the alternatives, the consumer can choose without incurring any cost.

It has already been mentioned that lack of full determinateness in governmental behaviour could arise from the government having only partial information on interpersonal utilities. A social welfare function has quite a few informational requirements and, in fact, if any of these is not fully met, it is possible that the government's preference will be incomplete. In the simplistic fashion in which the social welfare function is discussed in the standard and generalised models the informational requirements are not immediately obvious. Chapter 6 studies the various concepts which underlie a social welfare function, particularly the different concepts of measuring and comparing utilities. As far as the measurement of utility goes, discussions have usually clustered around cardinality and ordinality. We suggest some new measures which lie *between* cardinality and ordinality. Some standard types of interpersonal comparisons are also defined. We then explore the logical interconnections between these measurability and comparability types and comment on their relationships with different kinds of social welfare functions. This yields results which, it is hoped, will be of interest not only to the revealed preference analyst but also in other areas like the theory of risk and welfare economics in general. For instance, it is demonstrated that, even though the kinds of information about interpersonal utilities needed for utilitarian and equity-conscious social welfare functions[2] are different, given a particular assumption whenever the informational requirement of utilitarianism is satisfied

---

[1] Ogden Nash, *Everyone but Thee and Me*, p. 46, J. M. Dent & Sons Ltd, 1962.
[2] These terms are explained in Chapters 2 and 6.

the requirement for the equity-conscious welfare function is also auto-matically met.

The last part of Chapter 6 demonstrates how incompleteness in government preference could stem from utilities being 'quasi-cardinal' and interpersonal comparisons 'partial'. In particular it demonstrates the fact that partial comparability gives rise to very strong reasons why the types of incomparable projects discussed in Chapter 3 might arise in practice.

The political nature of government begins to emerge as we study interdependence between agents. Interdependence makes it possible that every agent chooses rationally but nevertheless the joint outcome is sub-optimal. Further complications arise if we introduce dynamic elements into this. An agent may then choose an alternative which is sub-optimal in the immediate context but through which he hopes to induce the others to behave in such a way in future that he makes an overall gain. What one agent expects the other to do in future may depend on intricate informational assumptions of high orders. Agent 1's knowledge of agent 2, and agent 1's knowledge of agent 2's knowledge of agent 1, etc. play an important part in agent 1's decision-making. What assumptions should the revealed preference analyst make about agent 1's knowledge? Chapter 7 discusses the simple and iterated Prisoner's Dilemma and uses it to illustrate some paradoxes of interdependence.

This game also helps one understand the existence of political constraints, which is the subject matter of Chapter 8. In order to evaluate an agent's preference it is necessary to know which of the rejected projects were feasible. The nebulous nature of political constraints makes it difficult to partition the set of rejected projects into feasible and infeasible ones. A more intractable difficulty arises from the fact that, often, of two projects which have the same ultimate characteristics (e.g. two projects which generate the same amounts of benefit to the same people) but have different ways of generating them (e.g. one through taxes and subsidies and the other through an irrigation scheme), political constraints may make one infeasible but not the other.

The final section of the book is concerned with some of the suggested uses of revealed weights. It pays particular attention to the use of value weights in cost–benefit analysis. Some of the broader issues regarding the relevance of revealed preference are discussed in the following section.

The question of governmental rationality is, in a sense, prior to the analysis of revealed preference. Hence, a brief introduction to this topic is provided in this chapter. A fuller discussion would, however, be better appreciated once some models of revealed preference have been considered and is therefore refrained from until Chapter 4.

Motivation

Planning involves value judgements. As Mera (1969) points out, 'public officials need some social welfare function, implicit or explicit, for formulating and administering policies and programs'. The process of planning could be thought of as involving two (usually implicit) steps. Firstly, the effects of different projects (e.g. a steel plant or an underground railway) have to be determined in terms of the types of social states created by them. Secondly, these states have to be ordered in accordance with the social welfare generated by them in order to facilitate a choice between the different projects. This latter step involves value judgements. Each social state will have its own level of unemployment, inflation, inequality, etc., and any comparison between different states necessitates judgements regarding the relative importance of these features. One possible source of value 'weights' is the government. And revealed preference algorithms are techniques for evaluating governmental value judgements (e.g. distributional weights). In recent years, awareness of this need to have value weights for planning and cost–benefit analysis has increased and, hence, it is not surprising that the Weisbrod (1968) and UNIDO (1972) models of evaluating government preference have received so much attention (Freeman, 1969; Musgrave, 1969; Mishan 1974; Little & Mirrlees, 1974). For an application of the UNIDO model see Datta Chaudhuri and Sen (1970).

Much of the interest in this subject derives from the controversy surrounding the role of normative judgements in planning. While some works like the UNIDO study argue in favour of using some limited political weights, there have been objections to this from many quarters. Mishan (1974) has been strongly critical of any use of political or governmental value judgements in cost–benefit analysis. We try to argue in Chapter 9 that his stand is untenable. The more general question about the use of revealed weights in cost–benefit analysis is also discussed in the same chapter.

Analysis of revealed preference models stimulates a discussion of wider issues in public economics which, besides being delightful exercises in themselves, also have a considerable practical relevance. Practical relevance, not in the sense of directly influencing policy decisions, but serving instead to expose the inherent fallacies in some widely held notions and helping to reshape ideas. This is often of greater consequence than one would expect.

Finally, welfare economics and planning have seen a proliferation of esoteric theories in recent times. It is a justifiable grievance of many that these theories have tended to remain abstruse, little attempt having been made to relate them to everyday facts. The present kind of enquiry provides an excellent opportunity to get some of these theories to bear upon more practical issues.

Governmental rationality

Many disparate areas of economics have tacitly employed the notion of a rational government – a government working towards certain economic objectives. But clearly, if our *homo oeconomicus* is suspect, a rational government is much more so. But before considering this issue, one needs to answer the more basic question of who comprises the government.

This is a much more complex question than may appear at first sight. But let us shelve these intricacies for the time being and look at the idealised model conceptualised in the UNIDO guidelines. In this model, the 'ministers' or the members of the ruling party are the government It is implicitly assumed that a unitary interest guides the ruling party, and, hence, we could think of the government as a single policy-making agent. It is assumed that projects are evaluated by project analysts (e.g. economists and technocrats) but the ministry, or government, is the ultimate decision-maker about the choice of projects. This is, of course, an unrealistic model. It is difficult, in reality, to say who makes the decisions. Power is diffused in many quarters and the government is a nebulous organisation. Moreover, far from having a unitary interest, the same government harbours many conflicting motivations.

As a prelude to the simple model in Chapter 2, we shall assume the simplistic notion of government employed by UNIDO. Later chapters examine this concept of government more closely and allow for the fact that there will, in reality, be intra-governmental conflicts and also that political constraints severely limit the role of the government as the ultimate decision-maker.

As far as governmental rationality goes, it is assumed in the UNIDO *Guidelines* and by Weisbrod that governments choose projects so as to maximise a weighted average of certain economic objectives. This is a strong rationality assumption, though to do it justice it should be noted that it does not mean that these motives guide governments in all spheres of decision-making. There will be many areas where non-economic aims get priority, but as far as project choice goes the government is assumed to be a maximiser of some social welfare function.

We begin by emulating the UNIDO and Weisbrod assumption that the choice of projects depends on the government and the government chooses so as to attain certain economic objectives. Based on this, we formalise the standard approach to evaluating governmental preference and later go on to examine this assumption.

2

The standard model in revealed preference theory

The simple revealed preference technique, which is constructed here and referred to as the standard model, is a formalisation of the models in UNIDO (1972) and Weisbrod (1968). These models have received considerable attention and use a concept of government fairly typical in economics. Consequently, they provide a convenient basic reference and stimulate questions which form the genesis of later chapters. But some spade work needs to be done before approaching the standard model and the next section contains a brief discussion of the social welfare function, which will be familiar terrain to many. The chapter ends with an analysis of the technical properties of the standard model, relegating proofs to an appendix, and comments on the UNIDO and Weisbrod approaches.

Social welfare functions

The purpose of a social welfare function (SWF) is to generate an ordering over the set of alternative social states. The sort of SWF which we shall be concerned with is a real-valued one. Let X be the set of alternative social states. A real-valued SWF attaches a number to each social state, x, contained in X. This number represents the welfare generated by this state x. The elements of X can then be ordered according to the welfare generated by each state.

Consider some standard SWFs. Given a utilitarian SWF, for any x contained in X, the welfare from x, $W(x)$, is the summation of the utilities of all the individuals in social state x. Hence, if we denote individual i's utility from state x as $U^i(x)$, then $W(x) = U^1(x) + \dots + U^n(x)$ assuming that there are n individuals. Social state y is declared superior to x if and only if $W(y) > W(x)$ or $\{U^1(y) - U^1(x)\} + \dots + \{U^n(y) - U^n(x)\} > 0$. Aggregation usually involves interpersonal comparisons and utilitarianism is no exception. For example, if $U^1(y) - U^1(x) = 2$, and $U^2(y) - U^2(x) = 1$, then we are saying that individual 1's increase in satisfaction in going from state x to y is twice that of individual 2. This is a *precise* interpersonal comparison and the validity of such comparisons has been debated (Robbins, 1938; Sen, 1970). As a prelude to a later discussion (Chapter 6) it may be observed that it has been argued that, while precise judgements (like 'twice') are dubious, one can make rough interpersonal comparisons. We can say that the increase in individual 1's utility is two to three times that of individual 2. Utilitarianism can be based on such rough judgements (Sen, 1970) though it may fail to generate complete orderings over the elements of X. For instance, we may be able to say that y is superior to x and z, but we may fail to compare x and z. This and other issues regarding the informational basis of SWFs are discussed in Chapter 6.

Another well known SWF is the Rawlsian type. According to this, for every x contained in X, $W(x) = \min U^i(x)$, i.e. welfare of social state x is equal to the utility of the worst-off individual in state x. The use of the term 'worst-off' clearly shows the need for interpersonal comparisons.

The common feature of the utilitarian and Rawl type SWFs is that, in both cases, we are given rules to derive social welfare from descriptions of individual *utilities* in different social states. But utilities are not observable and, for the planner attempting to order alternative states, what is needed are rules for deriving social welfare from the *observable* features of social states. An example of this is a SWF according to which $W(x)$ is the summation of the incomes of all citizens. This SWF is identical to the utilitarian one if individual utility is taken to be equivalent to individual income. But this SWF is unappealing and would probably fail to explain governmental behaviour. It implies that there is only one objective, namely, to augment aggregate income or consumption. Any government will have also a host of other objectives like improving income distribution and providing more 'merit goods'.

Consider the distribution objective. A simple way to introduce this into the SWF—a method adopted in UNIDO (1972)—is to split the citizens into s income groups, and set $W = a_1 Y_1 + \ldots + a_s Y_s$, where Y_i denotes income of group i, making sure that if group i is poorer than group j then $a_i > a_j$, i.e. the income of a poorer group is given a greater weight than that of a rich one.[1] If some Y_i increases, ceteris paribus, W increases. Hence, the aggregate objective is taken into account. Alternatively, if we consider a unit increase in the incomes of a rich group and a poor group, then, in the latter case, the increase in W is greater and this reflects the redistribution objective. There are two ways of viewing the above SWF: we could think of the government as having either two objectives— increasing and redistributing income; or s objectives—increasing the incomes of groups $1, 2, \ldots, s$ (with, of course, differential weighting).

A merit good is a commodity which is felt to be insufficiently demanded in the private market. A commonly cited example is education. A government may feel that a special stress ought to be laid on education. Such

---

[1] An alternative way of introducing equity considerations into the SWF is as follows: $W = f(Y, \sigma)$, $f_Y > 0$ and $f_\sigma < 0$, where Y is the aggregate income and σ some measure of inequality like the Gini coefficient.

an objective is easily introduced into the above SWF. Ignoring the problems of measurement, if E is the amount of education in an economy, then the welfare function may be augmented as follows: $W = a_1 Y_1 + \ldots + a_s Y_s + a_{s+1} E$, where $a_{s+1} > 0$. Other objectives—and there may be many (see Marglin, 1967; UNIDO, 1972)—may be introduced in a similar fashion.

It is important to note that the values of the coefficients $a_1, \ldots, a_{s+1}$ will not remain constant as conditions in the economy change. For example, as more education becomes available, a_{s+1} will become smaller. Hence, to write the SWF in its most general form, linearity has to be eschewed. Also, instead of writing $Y_1, \ldots, Y_s, E$, we could use the more general symbols $B_1, \ldots, B_k$, since we do not know what the government's actual objectives are. Hence, we adopt the general form of SWF:

$$W = F(B_1, B_2, \ldots, B_k) \qquad (2.1)$$

This implies that the government has k objectives. B_i will be called the amount of benefit i or (at the risk of grammatical deviation) the amount of objective i. It is important that $B_1, \ldots, B_k$ be *observable* features of an economy. What form the function F *should* have is a matter for welfare economics and ethics. The main concern of the revealed preference analyst is to try and discover the nature of the function F implied by an agent's behaviour.

Global and local social welfare functions

In the above function (2.1), the variables were aggregate amounts of the k objectives in the economy. Such a function is called the *global social welfare function* (GWF).

Assume that a project planner knows the GWF. He has to evaluate the social welfare generated by project p_j. Let B_i^j be the amount of benefit i generated by the project. Clearly he cannot substitute B_i^j for B_i in (2.1) in order to calculate the social welfare generated by the project, because (2.1) is a global function and B_i^j is the increase in benefit i caused by the project p_j and not the aggregate amount of i in the economy. Given that the project analyst has information only of the amounts of benefits (or objectives) generated by the projects he is evaluating and not of the aggregate situation of the economy, he needs an SWF, the arguments of which are increments to benefits rather than aggregate benefits.

Consider the following SWF:

$$W^j = g(B_1^j, B_2^j, \ldots, B_k^j) \qquad (2.2)$$

The arguments are now increments in benefits and W^j the consequent increase in welfare. Such a SWF is called a *local social welfare function*

(LWF). Given a GWF and a vector of aggregate benefits representing the state of the economy it will be possible to derive the LWF.

Assuming that the GWF is differentiable, take total differentials of (2.1):

$$dW = \frac{\delta F}{\delta B_1} dB_1 + \frac{\delta F}{\delta B_2} dB_2 + \dots + \frac{\delta F}{\delta B_k} dB_k \qquad (2.3)$$

$$\frac{\delta F}{\delta B_i} = f_i(\bar{B}), i = 1, \dots, k$$

where $\bar{B}$ is a k-element vector of aggregate objectives.

As long as the economy remains in the vicinity of a particular $\bar{B}$, for all practical purposes $\frac{\delta F}{\delta B_i}$ can be assumed to be constant. Such a vicinity of $\bar{B}$ is called a *locality*. And the space drawn with the origin at $\bar{B}$ is called the *local space* (see Figure 2.1). As long as the economy remains within a locality we could write $\frac{\delta F}{\delta B} = a_i$, where a_i is a constant. Writing W^j for dW and B_i^j for dB_i in (2.3) we get

$$W^j = a_1 B_1^j + a_2 B_2^j + \dots + a_k B_k^j \qquad (2.4)$$

This is an LWF, albeit an approximate one. A project planner's maximand could be expressed in the form of (2.4). If we have data on various project choices from different sets of projects, we can assume that (2.4) is the maximand as long as we can ensure that all the choices are made within the same locality.

Figure 2.1 illustrates a global and a local space in an economy with two objectives. In this diagram the economy is at (B_1^a, B_2^a). Hence for the project planner O' is the origin, and given that the projects are not too large, i.e. they lie within the local space, the indifference curves may be assumed to be linear. If the GWF is linear, then the GWF is identical to the LWF. It is, however, unlikely that any government would have a linear GWF.

Weisbrod (1968) uses a linear social welfare function. This can be misleading since he does not distinguish between LWFs and GWFs. The linearity assumption is justified only for an LWF. In the ensuing pages it is assumed that the projects are small and the economy remains within the confines of one locality. This permits the use of a linear LWF in the standard model below. Though the social welfare function is referred to simply as the SWF in the following sections, it should be clear that what we have in mind is the LWF.

It is important to note that though, given a GWF, LWFs may be derived from it, it is quite possible that a government does not have a GWF but has LWFs. This means that within each locality the govern-

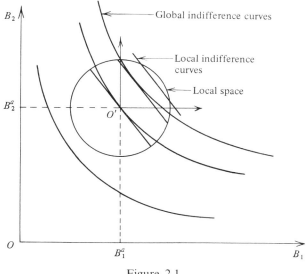

Figure 2.1

ment may have a consistent manner of behaving, though the behaviour in all localities assembled together may not reveal the existence of a GWF. This is in keeping with a view held by many government theorists that a government seldom has a global maximand, though given a particular situation it knows how to react (Lindblom, 1959). The standard model permits this sort of behaviour on the part of the government. By treating different localities separately, a considerable weakening of the rationality requirements of the government, compared to the Weisbrod (1968) model, is made possible.

The standard model

Let X be the set of all mutually exclusive and independently executable projects or project-combinations. An element of X is denoted by p_i. Though p_i may be a single project or a project-combination, it will be referred to as a project.

A project is typically not valued for its own sake but for its ability to achieve certain objectives (or, in other words, to generate certain benefits). Each project is a bundle of characteristics and can be represented by a k-element vector, such that the ith element of the vector represents the amount of benefit i generated by the project. The k-dimensional Euclidean space, E^k, with each axis representing the amount of an objective, will be called the *objective space* or the *O-space*. In the Weisbrod model each axis denotes the income of a particular group. Each project can be thought of as a point in the O-space. It is interesting to note that this definition of a project is similar to Lancaster's (1971) conception of a consumer good.

Formally, there exists a function $f : X \to E^k$. This function is not necessarily one-to-one since any $x \in O$-space may be the image of more than one $p_i \in X$. Because of indivisibilities and technological constraints, f is not necessarily an onto function.

It is assumed that the government evaluates some projects before selecting one. Kornai (1971) calls these the explored decision alternatives. One question which immediately arises is: how does the government decide which projects to evaluate? Also, given that evaluation is costly, is it always reasonable to evaluate projects before making a choice? These are simple questions at first sight but complexities multiply as one tries to answer them. Clearly, if the welfares generated by two alternative projects are not very different, evaluation is not worthwhile. But how does one know that the welfares generated are not very different before evaluation? This is an intricate problem and Chapter 5 looks into it. For the time being, assume that there is a set of evaluated projects. Of these, some will be feasible. Let us denote the set of evaluated and feasible projects by F. The government chooses a project from F, which is at least as good as each project in F in terms of the SWF of the government:

$$W = a_1 B_1 + a_2 B_2 + \ldots + a_k B_k \qquad (2.5)$$

where $W =$ social welfare, $B_i =$ objective of type i, and $a_i =$ weight on objective i. This is the same function as (2.4). It should be clear that a_i reflects the importance of one unit of objective i. The aim of revealed preference analysis is to discover the government's SWF, that is, to evaluate the k-element vector $\bar{a} = [a_1, a_2, \ldots, a_k]$. The bar on $\bar{a}$ will be dropped where there is no possibility of confusing it with a scalar.

The k-dimensional Euclidean space, E^k, with the ith axis representing a_i is called the *weight space* or *W-space*. We may impose the *a priori* restriction that $\bar{a} > 0$ (i.e. $a_i \geq 0$ for all i, and there exists $a_j > 0$). This restriction implies that the marginal utility of no objective is negative; and that it is positive for at least one objective. If the non-negative orthant of E^k, without the origin, is denoted by M^k, then this *a priori* restriction says that $\bar{a} \in M^k$.

Let there be n projects $p_1, p_2, \ldots, p_n$ from which the government chooses. In other words, F consists of n elements. B_j^i represents the amount of benefit j provided by project p_i and W^i is the welfare generated by p_i. The n projects can be represented by the following system of equations.

$$
\begin{aligned}
a_1 B_1^1 + a_2 B_2^1 + \ldots + a_k B_k^1 &= W^1 \\
a_1 B_1^2 + a_2 B_2^2 + \ldots + a_k B_k^2 &= W^2 \\
\vdots \qquad\qquad\qquad &\quad\ \vdots \\
a_1 B_1^n + a_2 B_2^n + \ldots + a_k B_k^n &= W^n
\end{aligned}
\qquad (2.6)
$$

Let p_1 be the only project selected by the government. This implies that $W^1 \geq W^i$, for all $i = 1, 2, \ldots, n$. Hence, we get the following system of inequalities.

$$a_1(B_1^1 - B_1^2) + a_2(B_2^1 - B_2^2) + \ldots + a_k(B_k^1 - B_k^2) \geq 0$$
$$a_1(B_1^1 - B_1^3) + a_2(B_2^1 - B_2^3) + \ldots + a_k(B_k^1 - B_k^3) \geq 0$$
$$\vdots \qquad\qquad\qquad\qquad\qquad\qquad\qquad \vdots \qquad (2.7)$$
$$a_1(B_1^1 - B_1^n) + a_2(B_2^1 - B_2^n) + \ldots + a_k(B_k^1 - B_k^n) \geq 0$$

Each of the above $(n - 1)$ inequalities is called a *rejection inequality*, and the entire system is called a *system of rejection inequalities*. The government's act of choosing one project from F reveals $(n - 1)$ choices over pairs. Every act of government choice provides us with a system of rejection inequalities. Given that the evaluating economist knows all the B_j^is, he can solve the system of inequalities and find the set within which the government's $\bar{a}$ must lie. This set is called the *solution set* and it is a subset of the W-space.

Each rejection inequality in (2.7) defines a closed half-space through the origin in the W-space. This is illustrated with an example later. The intersection of the $(n - 1)$ half-spaces in (2.7) is the solution set. It is easy to see why this is so. Consider the half-space described by the first inequality in (2.7). This half-space consists of all values of $\bar{a}$ with which the choice of p_1 over p_2 is consistent, i.e. all $\bar{a}$ for which $W^1 \geq W^2$. Similarly the second inequality generates a half-space which is consistent with the choice of p_1 over p_3. Obviously, the space which is common to both these half-spaces, i.e. their intersection, consists of all and only those values of $\bar{a}$ which are consistent with the choice of p_1 over both p_2 and p_3. Proceeding similarly it is easy to see that the intersection of all the half-spaces in (2.7) gives us the set within which $\bar{a}$ must lie for the government's choice of p_1, from the set of available projects, to be rational.

It is interesting to note that the intersection of the $(n - 1)$ half-spaces gives us a convex polyhedral cone (see Fenchel, 1953, Theorem 16). If we want to impose the *a priori* restriction that $\bar{a}$ lies within $M^k(M^k$ being defined as above) then the solution set is the intersection of this polyhedral cone with M^k. The solution set is therefore convex.

If the solution set is empty, then there does not exist any SWF like (2.5) which can explain the government's behaviour. The government is then described as irrational in this standard model. There, however, remain important issues about rationality which will be taken up in later chapters.

A certain amount of economy of expression is possible by normalising the SWF. If $a_1 > 0$, then we could normalise by setting $a_1 = 1$. Then the welfare function is as follows.

$$W = B_1 + a_2 B_2 + \ldots + a_k B_k \qquad (2.8)$$

This SWF is the same as (2.5), excepting that the units of measuring welfare are different. In (2.8) objective 1 is the unit of account. If this procedure is adopted then a_1 is set equal to 1 in (2.6) and (2.7) as well. The solution set can now be expressed as a subset of a $(k - 1)$ dimensional W-space, with the axes representing $a_2, a_3, \ldots, a_k$.

An example

Let there be three objectives, e.g. consumption, respectively, to the wealthy, to the middle-class and to the poor. There are three contending projects. The table below shows the benefits created by the different projects.

	B_1	B_2	B_3
p_1	2	3	2
p_2	3	2	0
p_3	1	1	4

Project 1 is selected by the government. The system of rejection inequalities, with the SWF normalised by setting $a_1 = 1$, is as follows:

$$-1 + a_2 + 2a_3 \geq 0 \qquad\qquad \text{(E1)}$$

$$1 + 2a_2 - 2a_3 \geq 0 \qquad\qquad \text{(E2)}$$

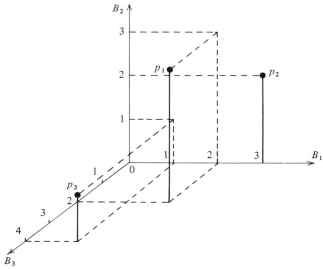

Figure 2.2

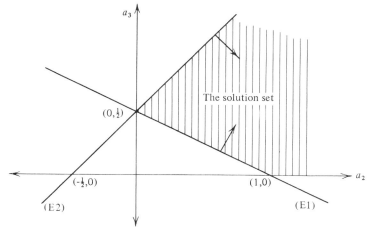

Figure 2.3

The two closed half spaces described by the above inequalities in the W-space, and the solution set are shown in Figure 2.3. These half-spaces do not pass through the origin, because we are using a normalised SWF. If (2.5) was used instead, then the W-space would be 3-dimensional and each half-space would pass through the origin.

The shaded region depicts the solution set. Note that $\bar{a} = [1, 1, 1]$ is an element of the solution set. Hence it is possible that the government does not attach any importance to the distribution of income.

If there are two solution sets, Ω^i and Ω^j, such that Ω^i is a proper subset of Ω^j, then Ω^i will be called *more efficient* than Ω^j. The choice of terminology is obvious. We are trying to locate the government's $\bar{a}$. From that point of view, Ω^i is superior to Ω^j: it is closer to hitting the mark and hence we call it more efficient. If the solution set consists of a single point in the $(k-1)$-dimensional W-space or a single ray through the origin in the k-dimensional W-space then the government's preference has been *exactly* revealed. Remember that k stands for the number of objectives in the government's SWF. It is worth noting that if $\bar{a}^*$ and $\bar{a}'$ are two points on the same ray through the origin in E^k, then whether we use $\bar{a}^*$ or $\bar{a}'$ in the SWF (2.5), the preferences over projects will remain unaffected. Hence, if we can get a solution set which is a single ray in the k dimensional W-space, then we have, in effect, revealed the government's preference exactly.

Till now we have only considered one system of rejection inequalities (i.e. a set of inequalities generated by the choice of *one* project). Now, assume that a government is observed to choose s times from s different sets of projects over a period of a few years. Provided that the economy has remained within one locality during this period, we could take the intersection of the *s* solution sets evaluated from the *s* systems of rejection inequalities and call it a *combined solution set*.

One should, however, be very careful in interpreting solution sets and combined solution sets. The former makes fewer demands on assumptions. If it were an empty set we could assert irrationality on the part of the government with much greater force than if the latter turned out to be empty. Over time an economy alters its position in the global *O*-space and the assumption of linearity of the SWF may be untenable. Moreover a government's preference may alter over time. All this may imply that the combined solution set which is the intersection of different solution sets will be an empty set; and from this to infer irrationality may not really be justified. When dealing with only one system of inequalities we are merely studying a government's preference at one point of time.

The strong ordering problem

Till now, it was being assumed that the selected project was *at least as good as* all the evaluated and feasible ones. However, in accordance with Samuelson's (1938) revealed preference theory, we could assume that the available projects are always strongly ordered, implying that the chosen project is *preferred* to all rejected, evaluated and feasible projects. This assumption has the advantage that every observation of choice would give us 'a definite piece of information about his preference ... Strong ordering gets off to a racing start; but even at the outset there are certain snags about it which deserve attention' (Hicks, 1956, p. 39). The main snag which Hicks demonstrated was the following. If we grant the assumption that commodities are divisible and a consumer's utility function is continuous[2] then it is logically necessary that there exist commodity bundles between which the consumer is indifferent. But even if we leave aside the snags discussed by Hicks, there remain some problems which tend to make the strong ordering assumption unacceptable.

Firstly, there is the much discussed introspective question. Does one always order alternatives strongly? The answer seems, at least to me, to be no. Secondly, there is a technically more interesting problem. Given the strong ordering assumption, we can no longer hope to find the 'exact' governmental weights, no matter how many rejection inequalities are available, assuming that the number of such inequalities is finite. The reason for this is obvious though the proof is less so. Given strong ordering, p_1 – the chosen project – is no longer merely *at least as good as* p_i;

---

[2] The assumption of a continuous utility function was not made in the original edition of Hicks (1956). This assumption is, however necessary and this was conceded by Hicks in a later edition. On this see Banerji (1964).

it is *better than* p_i. Hence, each rejection inequality is of the stronger form, i.e. $W^1 - W^i > 0$. This describes an *open* solution set in the O-space. As we use more and more rejection inequalities the solution set in the O-space shrinks but continues to remain an open set. Now, an open set can be empty but it can never contain a single point. Hence, we can never get to the exact governmental preference.

While the point being made is intuitively clear from the above, the present paragraph formalises the idea and may be skipped by less fastidious readers. Assume the government chooses project p_1 and rejects $p_2, \ldots, p_n$. Assuming strong ordering, the rejection inequalities are of the stronger form, i.e. $W^1 - W^i > 0$, for all $i \neq 1$. Each of these inequalities describes an open half-space in E^{k-1} (we are assuming a normalised SWF like (2.8)). Let the intersection of these half-spaces be C. The intersection of a finite number of open sets is open (see Nikaido, 1970, Theorem 12.2). Therefore, C is an open set. As before, we have the *a priori* restriction that $[a_2, \ldots, a_k] \in E_+^{k-1}$, where E_+^{k-1} is the non-negative orthant of E^{k-1}. Hence, the solution set is $C \cap E_+^{k-1}$. Let e be a $(k-1)$-element identity vector, i.e. $e = [1, 1, \ldots, 1]$. Let $x \in C \cap E_+^{k-1}$. Then for all $h > 0$, $x + he \in E_+^{k-1}$. Since C is an open set, we can choose some $h > 0$, say $\bar{h}$, such that $x + \bar{h}e \in C$. Hence, $x + \bar{h}e \in C \cap E_+^{k-1}$. Therefore, if $C \cap E_+^{k-1} \neq \phi$ (the empty set), then $C \cap E_+^{k-1}$ contains more than one element. In fact it will contain an infinite number of elements if it is not an empty set. Hence, exact governmental weights cannot be derived.

It is obvious that if two solution sets are evaluated from the same data, one assuming weak ordering and the other strong, then the latter will be more efficient than the former, i.e. the latter will be a proper subset of the former. In case the solution set based on weak ordering is a singleton, then the strong ordering solution set will be empty. This is obvious because the strong ordering solution set is the interior of the weak ordering one.

The existence of solution sets*

This section analyses the necessary and sufficient conditions for the existence of solution sets. We begin with some comments on terminology.

The vector $\bar{x}$ is said to *vector-dominate* (V-*dominate*) the vector $\bar{y}$ if and only if $x_i \geq y_i$, for all i and for some $j, x_j > y_j$. If $\bar{x}$ V-*dominates* $\bar{y}$, we write $\bar{x} > \bar{y}$.

$\bar{x}$ strictly V-*dominates* $\bar{y}$ if and only if $x_i > y_i$, for all i. If $\bar{x}$ strictly V-dominates $\bar{y}$, we write $\bar{x} \gg \bar{y}$.

$\bar{x}$ weakly V-*dominates* $\bar{y}$ if and only if $x_i \geq y_i$, for all i. If $\bar{x}$ weakly V-dominates $\bar{y}$, we write $\bar{x} \geq \bar{y}$.

In Figure 2.4, $\bar{e}$ strictly V-dominates $\bar{b}$, V-dominates $\bar{c}$ and weakly V-dominates $\bar{e}$. In fact the relation of weak V-domination is reflexive,

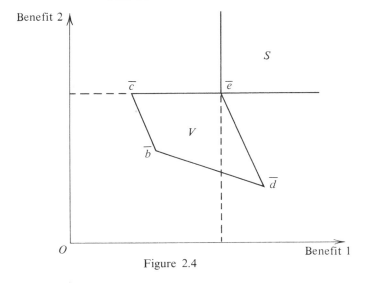

Figure 2.4

i.e. for all $\bar{x}$, $\bar{x}$ weakly V-dominates $\bar{x}$. Between $\bar{c}$ and $\bar{b}$ there is no domination either way.

The notion of 'existence' is simple and will be discussed here, while the proofs of the existence theorems are relegated to the appendix.

To begin with a simple case of non-existence of a solution set, consider two projects $\bar{B}^1$ and $\bar{B}^2$, such that $\bar{B}^2 \gg \bar{B}^1$. For visual illustration, we could think of $\bar{B}^2 = \bar{e}$ and $\bar{B}^1 = \bar{b}$ in Figure 2.4. If the government chooses $\bar{B}^1$ and rejects $\bar{B}^2$, then there is no negatively sloped indifference curve which can explain the government's choice. Hence the solution set (i.e. the set of all $\bar{a}$ which can explain the government's choice) is empty.

This can be more formally established as follows (this formality is useful only as a prelude to the proofs of theorems in the appendix): The choice of $\bar{B}^1$ over $\bar{B}^2$ gives the following rejection inequality,

$$a_1(B_1^1 - B_1^2) + a_2(B_2^1 - B_2^2) + \ldots + a_k(B_k^1 - B_k^2) \geq 0 \qquad (2.9)$$

Let Ω be the half-space in the k-dimensional W-space described by (2.9). Now, remembering that $\bar{B}^2 \gg \bar{B}^1$, it follows that for all $\bar{a} > 0$,

$$a_1(B_1^1 - B_1^2) + a_2(B_2^1 - B_2^2) + \ldots + a_k(B_k^1 - B_k^2) < 0$$

Hence, if $\bar{a} > 0$, then $\bar{a} \notin \Omega$, since Ω contains only those $\bar{a}$ which satisfy (2.9). This means that $\Omega \cap M^k$ (the solution set) $= \phi$. Remember that $M^k = \{\bar{x} \in E^k \mid \bar{x} > 0\}$

Consequently, if the government ever chooses a project which is strictly vector-dominated by a rejected project, we can straightaway declare the solution set to be empty. On the other hand, the rejection of a project which is strictly V-dominated by some other project gives us no information about government preference. In the above example, if the government had selected $\bar{B}^2$ rather than $\bar{B}^1$, then the half-space described by the rejection inequalities would contain the entire M^k, since such a choice is compatible with all negatively sloped indifference curves. Hence, the choice of $\bar{B}^2$ would give us no additional information regarding governmental preference.

We have just seen that a strictly vector-dominated project cannot be chosen by a rational government. But can a rational government choose any project that is not vector-dominated by any rejected project? The answer is in the negative and the example below demonstrates this.

An example

The table below describes three projects which have been evaluated and are feasible.

	B_1	B_2	B_3
p_1	1	1	1
p_2	0	2	4
p_3	4	2	0

If the government chooses p_1 then the two rejection inequalities, assuming that the SWF is normalised by setting $a_1 = 1$, are as follows:

$$1 - a_2 - 3s_3 \geq 0 \tag{E1'}$$

$$-3 - a_2 + a_3 \geq 0 \tag{E2'}$$

The half-spaces described by (E1') and (E2') are shown in Figure 2.5.

It is clear that the solution set is empty, in spite of the fact that $\bar{B}^1 \not< \bar{B}^2$ and $\bar{B}^1 \not< \bar{B}^3$ ('$\not<$' means 'does not dominate').

This example shows that the mere absence of vector-domination of the chosen project by any rejected one is not sufficient for the solution set to be non-empty. However, in the above example, while $\bar{B}^1$ is not dominated by $\bar{B}^2$ or $\bar{B}^3$, there is a convex combination of rejected projects which dominate $\bar{B}^1$. Note that $\bar{B}^1 \ll \frac{1}{2}\bar{B}^2 + \frac{1}{2}\bar{B}^3 = [2, 2, 2]$.

This is clear from Figure 2.4. Among the three projects, $\bar{b}$, $\bar{c}$ and $\bar{d}$, project $\bar{b}$ is dominated by no single project but by a combination of $\bar{c}$ and $\bar{d}$. And clearly no straight line indifference curve could lead to $\bar{b}$ being the best project. This is the intuition behind Theorem 2*2.

If however, a project is not strictly vector-dominated by any convex combination of the projects from which the choice is made, then there are SWFs which can explain the choice. An informal proof can be sketched immediately. Let the chosen project p_1 be represented by $\bar{e}$ in Figure 2.4.

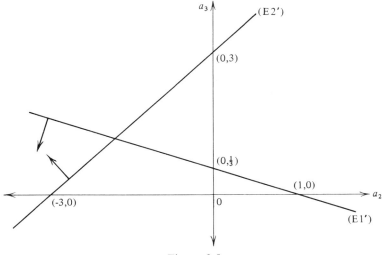

Figure 2.5

Let the convex hull of projects, $p_1, \ldots, p_n$, be denoted by V. In Figure 2.4 V is the convex hull of $\bar{b}, \bar{c}, \bar{d}$ and $\bar{e}$. Let S be the set of all those points in E^k which strictly V-dominate p_1. Since p_1 is not strictly V-dominated by any convex combination of the projects, there are no common points between V and S. And since both these sets are convex, there must exist a hyperplane at p_1 which separates V and S. This follows from a well-known theorem (see Theorem 30.1, Nikaido, 1970). This hyperplane may be treated as an indifference surface which explains the choice of p_1 from $p_1, \ldots, p_n$. This result is stated in Theorem 2*1 and the formal proof is given in the appendix to this chapter.

*Theorem 2*1* If $\bar{B}^1 \not\ll \alpha_1 \bar{B}^1 + \alpha_2 \bar{B}^2 + \ldots + \alpha_n \bar{B}^n$ for any $\bar{\alpha}$ such that $\alpha_i \geq 0$, for all i, and $\sum_{i=1}^{n} \alpha_i = 1$, then there exists $\bar{a} > 0$ such that $W^1 \geq W^i$, for all i, where $W^i = \bar{a} \bar{B}^i$.

The converse theorem is important and should be obvious from the above discussion.

*Theorem 2*2* If $\bar{B}^1 \ll \alpha_1 \bar{B}^1 + \alpha_2 \bar{B}^2 + \ldots + \alpha_n \bar{B}^n$ for some $\bar{\alpha}$ such that $\alpha_i \geq 0$, for all i, and $\sum_{i=1}^{n} \alpha_i = 1$, then there does not exist $\bar{a} > 0$ such that $W^1 \geq W^i$, for all i, where $W^i = \bar{a} \bar{B}^i$.

For evaluating government preference, Theorems 2*1 and 2*2 are very important, as they could help curtail a lot of unnecessary calculations.

Let an economist be provided with the data on a project choice by the government (i.e. he has descriptions of all elements of F and knows which one was chosen) and be asked to evaluate the implicit weights using the technique of the standard model. He should then, prior to applying the algorithm, check the following as it may render a lot of calculation redundant.

(1) If the chosen project is strictly V-dominated by some convex combination of the projects in F (the set of feasible and evaluated projects), then without any further calculations he should declare the solution set to be empty. This follows from Theorem 2*2.

(2) Before calculating the solution set he may check for those projects which are strictly V-dominated by convex combinations of the projects in F and discard them. The government's rejection of such projects does not add any information to what is available from the rejection of the other projects.

Relevant objectives

Till now, it has been assumed that the government's objectives are somehow known, though the weights attached to them are not. But if we are operating on previously chosen projects or dealing with a minister who cannot spell out the objectives but can choose, then *a priori* judgement is necessary in deciding what objectives are relevant. This immediately opens up the possibility that some objectives which are relevant to the government may get omitted by us. What effect will this have on our analysis of government preference?

The choice of a project which seems irrational when only k objectives are considered may turn out to be rational when one more objective is introduced, as the chosen project may be well endowed in terms of this last objective. In our terminology, a project, which is strictly V-dominated by a convex combination of the rejected projects, may cease to be strictly V-dominated if another dimension is added to the O-space.

In order to avoid the errors of omitting relevant objectives one should not arbitrarily increase the number of objectives, since this will make the solution set inefficient. This is explained below.[3]

Assume that, given three objectives, we apply the revealed preference technique of the standard model and get a solution set $ABCD$ (Figure 2.6) – a_1 being set equal to 1. Now, if we were to go through the same exercise by ignoring objective 3, it would merely amount to setting $a_3 = 0$ (since a_3 is the 'importance' of one unit of objective 3). Then our solution set would be the closed interval AB. So, if objective 3 is actually unimportant to the government, but the revealed preference

---

[3] For a geometric analysis of relevant 'characteristics' in the context of consumer theory see Lancaster (1971).

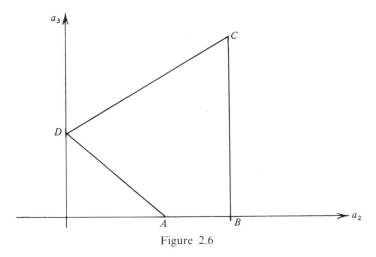

Figure 2.6

analyst considers it in applying the model, he will get an unnecessarily large solution set $ABCD$.

To explain this in the general case of k objectives, we have to resort to algebra. Let there be k objectives, and let the SWF be normalised by setting $a_1 = 1$. Then the system of rejection inequalities is as follows.

$$\begin{bmatrix} (B_2^1 - B_2^2) & (B_3^1 - B_3^2) \dots (B_k^1 - B_k^2) \\ (B_2^1 - B_2^3) & (B_3^1 - B_3^3) \dots (B_k^1 - B_k^3) \\ \vdots & \vdots \qquad\qquad \vdots \\ (B_2^1 - B_2^n) & (B_3^1 - B_3^n) \dots (B_k^1 - B_k^n) \end{bmatrix} \begin{bmatrix} a_2 \\ a_3 \\ \vdots \\ a_k \end{bmatrix} \geq \begin{bmatrix} -(B_1^1 - B_1^2) \\ -(B_1^1 - B_1^3) \\ \vdots \\ -(B_1^1 - B_1^n) \end{bmatrix} \qquad (2.10)$$

Let Ω^α be the solution set of this system. Let us assume, without loss of generality, that, in evaluating government preference, the last z objectives are ignored. Then the rejection inequality system will be as follows:

$$\begin{bmatrix} (B_2^1 - B_2^2) & (B_3^1 - B_3^2) \dots (B_{k-z}^1 - B_{k-z}^2) \\ (B_2^1 - B_2^3) & (B_3^1 - B_3^3) \dots (B_{k-z}^1 - B_{k-z}^3) \\ \vdots & \vdots \qquad\qquad \vdots \\ (B_2^1 - B_2^n) & (B_3^1 - B_3^n) \dots (B_{k-z}^1 - B_{k-z}^n) \end{bmatrix} \begin{bmatrix} a_2 \\ a_3 \\ \vdots \\ a_{k-z} \end{bmatrix} \geq \begin{bmatrix} -(B_1^1 - B_1^2) \\ -(B_1^1 - B_1^3) \\ \vdots \\ -(B_1^1 - B_1^n) \end{bmatrix} \qquad (2.11)$$

Let Ω^β be the solution set of this system. Solving this system is the same as solving (2.10) with $a_{k-z+1}, \dots, a_k$ set equal to zero. This means that if $[a_2^*, a_3^*, \dots, a_{k-z}^*] \in \Omega^\beta$, then if we add z zeros to the vector we get an element of Ω^α, i.e. $[a_2^*, a_3^*, \dots, a_{k-z}^*, 0, 0, \dots, 0] \in \Omega^\alpha$. Let $\Omega^{\beta 0}$ be the set containing exactly all elements of Ω^β with z zeros added to each vector. Then $\Omega^{\beta 0}$ is a proper subset of Ω^α. Hence, usually $\Omega^{\beta 0}$ is more efficient than Ω^α and Ω^α is never more efficient than $\Omega^{\beta 0}$.

All this raises certain fundamental questions about inferring preferences from choices. When analysing governmental choices in retrospect, there is clearly the possibility that some objectives which were of concern to the government get omitted by us. This could introduce errors into the evaluated preferences and also may make the solution set empty. For example, if the solution set displayed in Figure 2.6 had no common elements with the a_2-axis, then if we ignored objective 3 we would get an empty solution set. And if objective 3 *was* relevant to the government, then our charge of inconsistency would be baseless. If, on the other hand, we try to rule out this possibility by considering an arbitrarily large number of objectives, then our solution set is likely to become too large to be of much use.

This drives home the importance of determining the objectives of the government as accurately as possible, before applying revealed preference techniques. To do this is likely to require access to information beyond that directly related to projects, for example, government declarations and manifestos.

The Weisbrod and UNIDO approaches

Having constructed the standard model, which is a formalisation of the Weisbrod (1968) and UNIDO (1972) models, some comments on these approaches may now be of interest.[4]

Weisbrod's (1968) method 'rests on the assumption that all public projects which were adopted, despite their failure to meet cost–benefit criteria over a period, were adopted because of an implicit set of utility weights attached by the political process to the earnings of different income or regional groups' (Mishan, 1974, p. 88). It is proposed that, based on this assumption, we examine past project choices by the government and try to reveal a SWF which could justify them.

One immediate objection arises regarding Weisbrod's bold assumption that efficiency and distribution are the only two criteria for project choice. Any government will have 'merit want' objectives and political motives.[5] Haveman (1968) rightly points out that in the Weisbrod approach 'whatever influence political manipulation of the existence of non-quantifiable benefits or costs has on decision making ... is artificially attributed to the factor called "income redistribution"'.

As far as the classification of beneficiaries from projects is concerned, Weisbrod suggests that this 'could be arbitrarily' chosen. This does not make much sense as it is possible to alter the evaluated weights widely

[4] There have been other attempts to analyse government preferences by rather different methods. Mera (1969) suggested a technique based on the tax schemes of governments. A statistical model of finding the 'decision rule' of a government has been proposed by McFadden (1975).

[5] The effect of political motives on behaviour is discussed in Chapter 8.

by altering the groupings. Moreover, one extreme of an arbitrary grouping is to consider the entire set of beneficiaries as one group. This brings us right back to the framework where there are no distributional weights — a framework which Weisbrod rejects. The correct classification is the one which the government considers relevant.[6]

Unlike our simple model, Weisbrod does not try to find solution *sets* generated by rejection inequalities. Instead, he proposes some unjustifiable assumptions which alter the inequalities to equations and consequently he derives a solution *point* in the W-space. This is not only theoretically unacceptable but it creates its own technical problems. It introduces an identification problem: the necessity to match the number of equations with the number of objectives.

The UNIDO (1972) *guidelines* constructs a revealed preference model with the motivation of assimilating it into a general framework of planning. In the UNIDO model, the 'minister's' preference is not inferred from past choices. There is a dialogue between the planner and the minister. The latter is given a description of alternative projects. In our terminology, for every project p_j the benefit vector $\bar{B}^j$ is calculated and presented to the minister for him to choose. His preference is then analysed on the basis of his choice.

This model, being based on a 'dialogue' between the 'minister' and the planner who, in this case, is the person evaluating governmental weights, has an advantage in that the planner can point out any 'irrationality' in the minister's choice, thereby allowing him to reconsider his choice. On the other hand, leaving aside the practical problem of goading ministers to participate in dialogues, the main shortcoming of this model derives from the fact that it is based on *stated* preferences. It has some of the same weaknesses which surveys have. A verbal choice could differ from the actual choice (i.e. choice for implementation), for various reasons. Political constraints may be disregarded and actual preference may not be expressed for tactical reasons. Also, since this model is based on verbal choice anyway, there is no need to confine ourselves to actual projects. Given that the aim is to evaluate government preference, we may as well present the government with sets of imaginary projects, chosen so as to reveal its exact preference quickly.

These models have received considerable attention elsewhere (see Haveman, 1968; Freeman, 1969; Musgrave, 1969; Mishan, 1974), and we shall comment on them further as we go along.

Appendix to Chapter 2

Theorem 2*1 If $\bar{B}^1 \not\ll \alpha_1 \bar{B}^1 + \alpha_2 \bar{B}^2 + \ldots + \alpha_n \bar{B}^n$ for any $\bar{\alpha}$ such that

---

[6] Weisbrod is aware of this and this makes his suggestion of arbitrary grouping all the more surprising.

$\alpha_i \geq 0$, for all i, and $\sum_{i=1}^n \alpha_i = 1$, then there exists $\bar{a} > 0$ such that $W^1 \geq W^i$, for all i, where $W^i = \bar{a}\bar{B}^i$.

Proof [7] Define Q as the set of all points in E^k which are weakly V-dominated by any convex combination of $\bar{B}^1, \ldots, \bar{B}^n$. The proof is divided into four parts.

(1) We first prove that Q is a convex set.

Let V be the set of all convex combinations of the n projects. Let $\bar{x}^i$, $\bar{x}^k \in Q$. Then there exist $\bar{y}^i$, $\bar{y}^k \in V$ such that $\bar{x}^i \leq \bar{y}^i$ and $\bar{x}^k \leq \bar{y}^k$. Hence, for any $0 \leq \beta \leq 1$, $\beta\bar{x}^i \leq \beta\bar{y}^i$ and $(1-\beta)\bar{x}^k \leq (1-\beta)\bar{y}^k$. It follows $\beta\bar{x}^i + (1-\beta)\bar{x}^k \leq \beta\bar{y}^i + (1-\beta)\bar{y}^k$. But $\beta\bar{y}^i + (1-\beta)\bar{y}^k \in V$, since V is convex. Consequently $\beta\bar{x}^i + (1-\beta)\bar{x}^k \in Q$. Hence, Q is a convex set.

(2) Now we prove the existence of a separating hyperplane at $\bar{B}^1$.

Since $\bar{B}^1 \not\ll \alpha_1\bar{B}^1 + \alpha_2\bar{B}^2 + \ldots + \alpha_n\bar{B}^n$ for any $\bar{\alpha}$ such that $\sum_{i=1}^n \alpha_i = 1$ and $\alpha_i \geq 0$, for all i, there does not exist $\bar{x} \in Q$ such that $\bar{B}^1 \ll \bar{x}$. Hence $\bar{B}^1$ is not an interior point of Q. By the Minkowski theorem (Debreu, 1959, p. 25) there exists a hyperplane $H = \{\bar{x} \mid \bar{x}\bar{v} = p\}$, through $\bar{B}^1$ which bounds Q. Without loss of generality assume H to be such that for all $\bar{z} \in Q, \bar{z}\bar{v} \leq p$.

(3) We now prove that $\bar{v} > 0$.

Assume there exists $v_j < 0$. Let $\bar{y}$ be such that $y_i = B_i^1$, $i \neq j$ and $y_j < B_j^1$. Then $\bar{y} \in Q$ and $\bar{v}\bar{y} > \bar{v}\bar{B}^1 = p$. But this is impossible (see (2) above). Hence $\bar{v} > 0$.

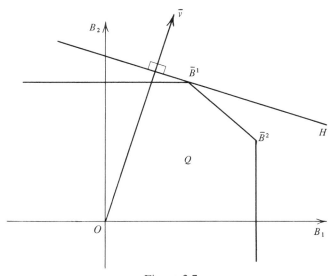

Figure 2.7

[7] This proof is based on the well-known Minkowski separation theorem. A shorter proof is possible by using Theorem 30.1 in Nikaido (1970), which is a variant of Minkowski's fundamental proposition.

(4) Let $W^i = \bar{a}\bar{B}^i$ be such that $\bar{a} = \bar{v}$. Then $\bar{a} > 0$ and $W^1 \geq W^i$, for all $i = 1, \ldots, n$.

Theorem 2*2 If $\bar{B}^1 \ll \alpha_1 \bar{B}^1 + \alpha_2 \bar{B}^2 + \ldots + \alpha_n \bar{B}^n$ for some $\bar{\alpha}$ such that $\alpha_i \geq 0$, for all i, and $\sum_{i=1}^n \alpha_i = 1$, then there does not exist any $\bar{a} > 0$ such that $W^1 \geq W^i$, for all i, where $W^i = \bar{a}\bar{B}^i$.

Proof Let $\bar{B}^1 \ll \alpha_1 \bar{B}^1 + \alpha_2 \bar{B}^2 + \ldots + \alpha_n \bar{B}^n$, for some $\bar{\alpha}$, such that $\alpha_i \geq 0$, for all i and $\sum_{i=1}^n \alpha_i = 1$. Hence, for any k-element vector $\bar{a} > 0$,

$$\bar{a}\bar{B}^1 < \alpha_1 \bar{a}\bar{B}^1 + \alpha_2 \bar{a}\bar{B}^2 + \ldots + \alpha_n \bar{a}\bar{B}^n$$

This implies that there exists t such that $\bar{a}\bar{B}^1 < \bar{a}\bar{B}^t$. Hence, there does not exist $\bar{a} > 0$ such that $W^1 = \bar{a}\bar{B}^1 \geq \bar{a}\bar{B}^i = W^i$, for all $i = 1, \ldots, n$.

3

Quasi-determinate government preference: a generalised model

A government is a heterogeneous body. Opinions vary among its sub-groups and the balance of power between these sub-groups frequently changes. Also, government decision-making involves interpersonal comparisons and it is possible that governments can make such comparisons only 'partially'. Thus, to expect a government to behave as consistently as was required in the previous chapter, and to brand it irrational if it fails to comply, is certainly an unreasonable demand. 'Weisbrod's illustration leaves no room for an "error" term', observes Chase (1968, p. 24). We set out now to construct a model which allows the government some room for 'errors'. In the generalised model the government is not required to have precise weights. Instead a weight could be expressed as a range, like, for instance, a bird in the hand is worth *two to three* in the bush. This, among other things, implies that the simple textbook illustration of indifference curves will no longer suffice.

This approach is designed to accommodate a wide range of behaviour. The standard model of the previous chapter and, hence, the UNIDO and Weisbrod approaches, are demonstrated to be a special case of the generalised model. This model is based on more realistic assumptions and is a considerable improvement on the traditional approach. However, even here we consider the government to be a *rational agent*, though a very weak form of rationality is required. A more fundamental criticism, as we shall see in later chapters, would challenge this.

We begin here with the problem of perceptional haziness. It is demonstrated how this could imply a lack of precision in government preferences. The effect of a limited inter-departmental conflict within the government is discussed later. These are only two examples of the many factors which give rise to the sort of indeterminateness which the generalised model allows. The effect of partial interpersonal comparisons is analysed in Chapter 6.

The problem of indifference

While the notion of indifference is treated as a simple and an obvious one in textbooks on economics, this has given rise to many interesting controversies. A notable contribution was made by Armstrong (1939), who argued that indifference was not 'transitive' and a major weakness of the Lausanne approach[1] was that it necessitated transitivity. We traverse these controversial grounds mainly with a view to criticising the standard model, which is based on the Lausanne framework, and motivating a generalised approach.

Let X be the set of all alternatives. Consider two alternatives x and y such that it does not matter to an agent which one he chooses, i.e., as far as choice goes, he has no reason to prefer one to the other. We shall then say that he is *neutral*[2] between x and y, and this is written as xNy. Let $N(x)$ be the set of exactly all those elements of X between which and x the agent is neutral. Hence, $y \in N(x)$ if and only if xNy is true. Formally, $N(x) = \{y \mid y \in X \text{ and } xNy\}$ and we refer to $N(x)$ as a *neutral class*. We assume what seems intuitively valid, that the relation of neutrality, N, is reflexive (i.e. for all $x \in X$, xNx) and symmetric (i.e. xNy implies yNx, for any $x, y \in X$).[3] For any $y \notin N(x)$, either y is preferred to x or x is preferred to y. It is assumed throughout that if a social state w is preferred to z, then given a choice between w and z, w will be chosen.

How do we interpret a neutral class, $N(x)$, in terms of utility or welfare? Various ideas have been proposed and we take a look at some of these.

According to the Lausanne school (see Armstrong, 1939) and Hicks (1939), one is neutral regarding choice between two alternatives if and only if the welfares from the two are the same: $xNy \leftrightarrow W(x) = W(y)$. This interpretation of neutrality implies that N is transitive, i.e. xNy and yNz implies xNz. This is easy to see. xNy and $yNz \rightarrow W(x) = W(y) = W(z) \rightarrow xNz$.[4]

Armstrong (1939) started from the premise that the relation of neutrality is not transitive. This can be demonstrated with an example. Consider a man who prefers a 1 mile evening-walk to a 2 mile one. It is quite possible and, in fact, very likely that he will be neutral between walks which are 1 mile plus n feet and 1 mile plus $n + 1$ feet. This implies a violation of transitivity because we can add one foot at a time to 1 mile and arrive at 2 miles. This led Armstrong to eschew the Lausanne interpretation. His explanation of neutrality was different. He argued that human perception was not knife-edged and hence, xNy did not imply that the utilities of x and y are exactly equal but merely that they are very close.

There are many interesting criticicms of Armstrong's argument. The Armstrong interpretation of the evening-walk example above has some difficulties. His interpretation implies that if we keep comparing a one

---

[1] This is discussed below.
[2] We reserve the term 'indifference' for a special case of neutrality. What we call 'neutral' here is similar to the traditional concept of indifference.
[3] The concept of a 'relation' is explained at length in Chapter 4.
[4] The symbols $\leftrightarrow$ and $\rightarrow$ denote 'if and only if' and 'implies that' respectively.

mile walk with successively a 1 mile 1 foot walk, a 1 mile 2 feet walk, and so on, then the individual will be neutral for some time, but at some point this neutrality will change to a strict preference. This seems unlikely and Fishburn (1970) points out how 'fuzziness' in human preference implies that there may not be any well defined point where neutrality changes to strict preference. This observation focuses on a logical difficulty which is similar to that in the Heap paradox. This age old paradox, due to the fourth century BC Greek philosopher Eubulides, points out that from a heap of grains, if one grain is removed at a time, then though there is no precise point at which it will change from a heap to a non-heap, it clearly will cease to be a heap after some time. Though we shall not discuss this difficulty, it is worth noting that one solution may lie in allowing preferences to be incomplete over some alternatives.

Another criticism of Armstrong arises from the fact that an agent may have no idea about the values of $W(x)$ and $W(y)$. For this agent, neither the relation of strict preference nor indifference holds between x and y, i.e. these states are non-comparable or his preference is incomplete over x and y. Under these circumstances, given a choice between x and y, he is very likely to be neutral between the two, i.e. xNy. Hence, from xNy, to make the Armstrong inference that $W(x)$ and $W(y)$ are close to each other may be fallacious. This has been persuasively argued by Majumdar (1958) (also see Sen, 1973a). This suggests a third interpretation, according to which xNy holds if and only if (a) $W(x)$ and $W(y)$ are very close, a special case of which is identity, or (b) preference over x and y is incomplete. This is a generalisation of Armstrong's analysis, and for brevity we refer to this as the Armstrong approach.

While the standard model was cast in the Lausanne framework, we adopt the Armstrong approach here. It will be assumed that if $W(x) = W(y)$ then xNy but not necessarily the other way round, because xNy could hold even if $W(x)$ and $W(y)$ were very close (Armstrong) or $W(x)$ and $W(y)$ were unknown to the decision-maker (Majumdar).

For any $x \in X$, let the set of all alternatives which generate exactly the same welfare as x be called an *indifference class* and be denoted by $I(x)$. Hence, $I(x) = \{y \mid y \in X \text{ and } W(y) = W(x)\}$. It is clear that according to the Lausanne school $I(x) = N(x)$, for all $x \in X$, whereas the Armstrong approach assumes $I(x) \subset N(x)$, for all $x \in X$.

The terminology used here differs from that of Armstrong. What is called the neutral class here, was called the indifference class by Armstrong. He had no special name for $I(x)$ – the set of iso-welfare alternatives – which we call the indifference class.

That the standard model was based on the Lausanne assumptions is easy to see. Let x be a point in the local O-space as in Figure 3.1. The indifference class at x, $I(x)$, was assumed to be linear and for any point y, which was not an element of $I(x)$, either y was preferred to x or x

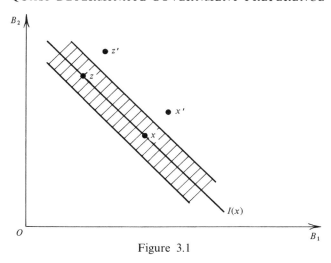

Figure 3.1

preferred to y, i.e. the choice between x and y was considered determined. In other words, it was assumed that $N(x) = I(x)$.

Now, consider the government whose indifference curves are still linear but $I(x)$ is a proper subset of $N(x)$. What would $N(x)$ look like? Majumdar (1958) represented $N(x)$ as a band around $I(x)$, as shown by the striped region in Figure 3.1. According to Majumdar's treatment if $y \in I(x)$ then $N(y) = N(x)$. This, it ought to be noticed, does not follow automatically from Armstrong's theory.

Is this a good representation? Let x in Figure 3.1 stand for $[10, 10]$, i.e. 10 units of B_1 and 10 units of B_2. Let $z = [8, 12]$ be an element of $I(x)$. Consider $x' = [11, 11]$ and $z' = [9, 13]$. If the government's perception was perfect then it would clearly see that both x' and z' are preferable to x since they dominate respectively $[10, 10] = x$ and $[8, 12] = z$. If however, its perceptions are slightly hazy, then which of x' and z' is more likely to be neutral to x? It intuitively seems to be z'. z' vector-dominates a point which is indifferent to x, whereas x' directly dominates x. It seems possible to argue that as one moves further away from x, along $I(x)$, the band of $N(x)$ would get broader.

A similar implication could be drawn from Fishburn's (1970) example: 'You are going to buy a car. You have no definite preference between (Ford, at \$2600) and (Chevrolet, at \$2700), and have also no definite preference between (Ford, at \$2600) and (Chevrolet, at \$2705). However, (Chevrolet, at \$2705) $\prec$ (Chevrolet, at \$2700).'[5]

In the light of these observations, a more realistic representation of

<hr>

[5] The symbol $\prec$ represents preference. $x \prec y$ implies y is preferred to x.

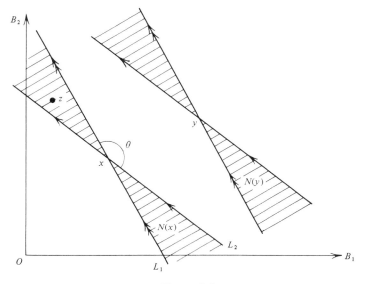

Figure 3.2

$N(x)$ would be the closed shaded region bounded by L_1 and L_2 in Figure 3.2.

Precisely how wide $N(x)$ is may be specified in terms of θ – the degree of precision. It is assumed that there exists a linear indifference curve (generated by a linear SWF as used in chapter 2) through x, inside $N(x)$, but its precise location is not known.

If we want to know the neutral region for any other point, e.g. y, we merely have to draw lines parallel to L_1 and L_2, through y. $N(y)$ is depicted by the striped region in Figure 3.2.

The area north-east of $N(x)$ represents the superior zone with respect to x. Any point in this zone is preferred to x; and consequently it is assumed that, given a choice between any point in the superior zone and x, the former is selected. Similarly, the south-west of $N(x)$ represents the inferior zone, and given a choice between any point in the inferior zone and x, x is always selected.

This sort of a representation will be extremely suitable for the case where the lack of full determinateness in the government's preference is caused by its inability to compare interpersonal welfares fully. In case B_1 and B_2 are the welfares to individuals 1 and 2 respectively and given that the government can only partially compare (Sen, 1970) their welfare, the neutral zones will be as in Figure 3.2, under some plausible assumptions. Why this is the case will be explained in Chapter 6, after we have studied the problems of interpersonal comparisons of utility.

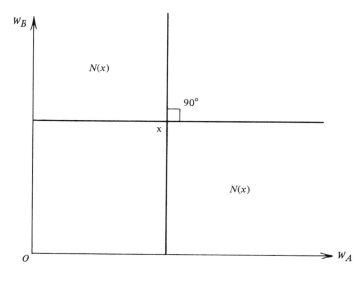

Figure 3.3

This representation implies that N is reflexive and symmetric, but not transitive – excepting in the limiting case where $N(x)$ is a line, i.e. $\theta = 180°$. It is no longer the case that $y \in I(x)$ implies $N(x) = N(y)$.

By suitably selecting θ, the dominance approach, of which the Pareto criterion is an example, and the linear neutral region approach of the standard model can be demonstrated to be special cases of this generalised representation.

A planner committed to the Pareto criterion and nothing else, choosing in a 2-dimensional space representing welfares to individuals A and B, has neutral zones such that $\theta = 90°$ as shown in Figure 3.3.

If $\theta = 180°$, then $N(x)$ is a straight line and since $I(x) \subset N(x)$, and $I(x)$ is a straight line, therefore $I(x) = N(x)$ and we are back to the framework of Chapter 2.

Assuming that governments have neutral zones of the nature discussed above, how do we apply revealed preference techniques? In the next section a 2-dimensional analysis is provided as a prelude to the k-dimensional case.

The generalised model in 2-dimensions

For revealed preference analysis an *a priori* degree of precision, θ, has to be chosen. Let $\theta = 150°$. A government is assumed to choose p_1 and reject p_2 in Figures 3.4 and 3.5.

Certainly the government could have an indifference curve which is

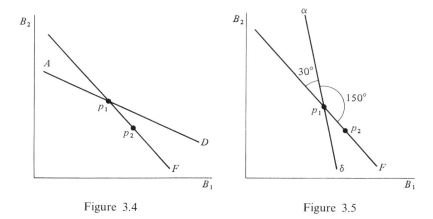

Figure 3.4   Figure 3.5

flatter than F. If this is not directly obvious, then consider an indifference curve AD, which is flatter than F, through p_1. If AD is the government's indifference curve, then AD must lie within $N(p_1)$. Now, since p_2 was rejected, p_2 cannot be in the superior zone to p_1. Clearly AD can satisfy this criterion. For any $N(p_1)$ containing AD, p_2 either lies in $N(p_1)$ or in the zone inferior to p_1. It cannot lie in the superior zone since the superior zone is in the north-east side of AD.

What about indifference curves steeper than F? It will be seen that indifference curves steeper than F by up to $30° = 180° - 150°$ are compatible with the act of choosing p_1 and rejecting p_2. $\alpha\delta$ in Figure 3.5, drawn through p_1 is $30°$ steeper than F. This $\alpha\delta$ is a possible indifference curve since it is possible to have a neutral zone $N(p_1)$ of degree of precision $150°$ which contains $\alpha\delta$ and also p_2. This means that under these circumstances, it is possible for p_2 not to be in p_1's superior zone.

However, if an indifference curve is any steeper than $\alpha\delta$, then for all $N(p_1)$ of degree of precision $150°$, which contain the indifference curve, p_2 must lie in the superior zone. Hence, the solution set contains all indifference curves like $\alpha\delta$ or flatter than $\alpha\delta$.

In Chapter 2, we would have concluded that only indifference curves flatter than F are possible. In the W-space, the solution set would then be a half-space like the shaded region in Figure 3.6. The solution set under the present algorithm is larger. It is the region on the left of SOS' in Figure 3.6. If we want to have the a priori restriction that $a_1 > 0$, $a_2 > 0$, as is implicit in some of the statements above, then the solution set is the intersection of the unrestricted solution set depicted in Figure 3.6 with the positive orthant.

It is intuitively obvious that the solution set is larger, the smaller the assumed degree of precision. A person using this algorithm is free to

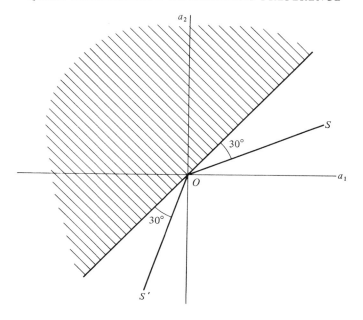

Figure 3.6

choose the degree of precision, keeping in mind that if he chooses a degree higher than what the government's actual degree of precision happens to be, then his solution set may be erroneous. If, on the other hand, he chooses a degree which is very small, then while he may be sure that the solution set contains the government's actual solution point, $\bar{a}$, the solution set will tend to be so large that it will not be very informative.

The generalised model, as enunciated above, has a serious shortcoming. Till now we have been dealing with a case where the government chooses one project from a pair. Now assume that there are n projects, $p_1, p_2, \ldots, p_n$, and the government chooses p_1. How do we find the solution set? This choice may be thought of as $n - 1$ indirect choices, which involve choosing p_1 from $\{p_1, p_2\}, \{p_1, p_3\}, \ldots, \{p_1, p_n\}$. In the standard model a simple method was used. For each choice the solution set was evaluated and the intersection of these solution sets was the solution set of the choice of p_1 from the set $\{p_1, p_2, \ldots, p_n\}$. This method, however, does not work in the generalised case. This is a serious and counter-intuitive problem. Let us state it formally.

Let $\bar{\Omega}$ be the set of $\bar{a}$ (and, by extension, the set of indifference curves) compatible with the choice of p_1 from $\{p_1, p_2, \ldots, p_n\}$, i.e. $\bar{\Omega}$ is the solution set. Let Ω^i be the set of $\bar{a}$ compatible with the choice of p_1 from $\{p_1, p_i\}$.

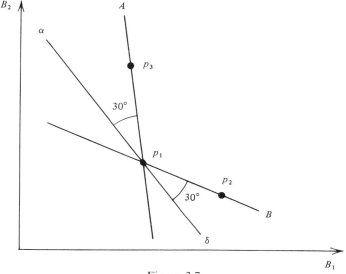

Figure 3.7

In the standard model,

$$\bar{\Omega} = \Omega^2 \cap \Omega^3 \cap \dots \cap \Omega^n = \bigcap_{i=2}^{n} \Omega^i$$

Models which satisfy this equality will be said to satisfy the *binary reconstruction property*. In the generalised model, where the government is allowed some degree of imprecision, this property is not, in general, satisfied. This is easily demonstrated with an example.

Let there be three projects p_1, p_2 and p_3 as shown in Figure 3.7. Let $\alpha\delta$ be $30°$ away from lines A and B respectively. The government selects project p_1 and rejects p_2 and p_3. We assume the degree of precision is $150°$ (i.e. imprecision is $30°$). As far as the choice of p_1 over p_2 is concerned $\alpha\delta$ is a possible indifference curve, by the above argument. Similarly $\alpha\delta$ is compatible with the choice of p_1 over p_3. However, $\alpha\delta$ is not compatible with the choice of p_1 over p_2 *and* p_3 ! This is so because no neutral zone with $30°$ imprecision can be drawn at p_1 such that neither p_2 nor p_3 are in the superior zone. So if $\bar{\Omega}$ is the set of all $\bar{a}$ compatible with the choice of p_1 from $\{p_1, p_2, p_3\}$ and Ω^2 and Ω^3 are the sets of $\bar{a}$ compatible with the choice of p_1 from $\{p_1, p_2\}$ and $\{p_1, p_3\}$ respectively, then we have just demonstrated how there may exist $\bar{a}$ (in our case the $\bar{a}$ associated with $\alpha\delta$) such that $\bar{a} \in \Omega^2 \cap \Omega^3$ but $\bar{a} \notin \bar{\Omega}$.

Though this may seem counter-intuitive at first, the cause of this problem is simple. This indifference curve $\alpha\delta$ permits the choice of p_1 over p_2 only by allowing $30°$ of error in a particular direction. For the choice of p_1 over p_3, $\alpha\delta$ is a possible indifference curve but this time with an error of $30°$ in the opposite direction. Hence, for $\alpha\delta$ to be compatible with the choice of p_1 over *both* p_2 and p_3, the error allowance has to be at least up to $60°$. But since we have permitted imprecision up to $30°$ only, $\alpha\delta$ fails to qualify.

In the face of this difficulty, how do we evaluate solution sets when a government chooses one project from more than two alternatives, or chooses more than one project? Fortunately a minor doctoring of the generalised model restores the binary reconstruction property. This is done by switching our search from possible indifference curves to possible neutral zones. Then the solution set will no longer be a set of possible indifference curves but it will be a set of possible neutral zones. Instead of doing this here, we make this alteration directly in the k-dimensional case considered below. Once this alteration is made we could first consider the government's choices over pairs, evaluate the associated solution sets, and then take their intersection to get the final solution set.

It is worth noting that though in developing this model we spoke of indifference (iso-welfare) and neutral classes, the existence of indifference classes is not essential for the generalised model to function. It is quite possible that no numerical welfare functions can be used to represent the government's preference. All we need is that the neutral zones are as suggested by Figure 3.2.

Now, we proceed to generalise the 2-dimensional representation of neutrality to k-dimensions and to make corresponding generalisations in the revealed preference technique. But before that a brief look is taken at some special types of cones.

Some special cones*

Let E^k be a k-dimensional Euclidean space. A *convex cone*, C, is a subset of E^k such that if $x, y \in C$, then $\lambda x + \mu y \in C$, for all $\lambda, \mu \geq 0$. A cone consisting of a non-zero vector x and all and only its multiples $\lambda x (\lambda \geq 0)$ is called a *ray*. A ray through x is denoted by (x). Note $(x) = (\lambda x)$ if $\lambda > 0$.

A metric for the rays in E^k may be defined as follows (see Fenchel, 1953):

$$[x, y] = \left(2 - \frac{2x'y}{\|x\|\,\|y\|} \right)^{1/2}$$

This metric is the chord distance between two points $x/\|x\|$ and $y/\|y\|$ on the unit sphere $\|z\| = 1$. That is $[x, y] = d\left(\dfrac{x}{\|x\|}, \dfrac{y}{\|y\|} \right)$. Note that $\left\| \dfrac{x}{\|x\|} \right\| = 1$, for all $x \neq 0$.

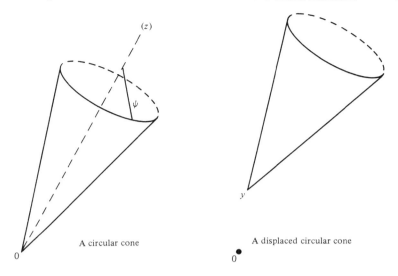

Figure 3.8

The σ-neighbourhood, $C(x, \sigma)$ of $(x) \subset E^k$ is defined as follows:

$$C(x, \sigma) = \{y \,|\, [x, y] < \sigma\}$$

If K is a convex cone such that $K \neq E^k$ and for some ray (z) and real number $\psi > 0$, $K = C(z, \psi)$ then K is called a *circular cone*.

For any $y \in E^k$, the set $\{y\} + C(x, \sigma) = C'(y, x, \sigma)$ is called a *displaced circular cone* at y, given that $C(x, \sigma)$ is a circular cone.[6] Figure 3.8 shows a circular cone and a displaced circular cone in E^3. In these diagrams and others the axes will not be drawn. The reader should imagine the necessary axes.

If $X \subset E^k$, then we define $-X$ as $\{x \,|\, -x \in X\}$. If $C(x, \sigma)$ is a circular cone then the set $T(x, \sigma) = \{E^k \backslash \{C(x, \sigma) \cup - C(x, \sigma)\}\} \cup \{0\}$ will be called a *cone complement*.[7] It should be noted that a cone complement is *not* the complement of a cone but the union of the set containing just the origin and the complement of a special type of cone. A cone complement is itself a cone. For any $y \in E^k$, the set $\{y\} + T(x, \sigma) = T'(y, x, \sigma)$ is called a *displaced cone complement* at y, given that $T(x, \sigma)$ is a cone complement. Since $T(x, \sigma) = T'(0, x, \sigma)$, it is clear that a cone complement is a special case of a displaced cone complement (and similarly for a circular cone since $C(x, \sigma) = C'(0, x, \sigma)$). When there is no possibility of ambiguity the term 'displaced' will be dropped from displaced circular cone and displaced cone complement, for the sake of brevity. The letters C and T will

---

[6] Given $S, T \subset E^k$, the set $S + T$ is defined as $\{x + y \,|\, x \in S, y \in T\}$.
[7] For any two sets X and Y, $X \backslash Y$ is the *relative complement* of Y in X, i.e. $X \backslash Y = \{x \in X \,|\, x \notin Y\}$.

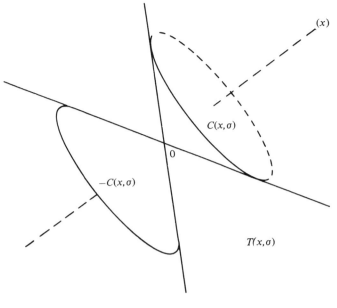

Figure 3.9

usually be reserved for circular cones and cone complements respectively. Figure 3.9 depicts a cone complement in E^3.

For any $x \in E^k$ and real number σ, if there exists a cone complement $T(x, \sigma)$ then this cone complement and the pair of circular cones $C(x, \sigma)$ and $- C(x, \sigma)$ will be said to be *associated* with one another.

If $H = \{x \mid x'a = 0\}$ is a hyperplane, then $H^+ = \{x \mid x'a \geq 0\}$ and $H^- = \{x \mid x'a \leq 0\}$.

Some lemmas are now stated in order to clarify and formalise certain relevant properties of cones. The proofs are contained in the appendix.

Lemma 1 If $H = \{x \mid x'a = 0\}$ is a bounding hyperplane for the circular cone C, then it must be a bounding hyperplane for $- C$. C and $- C$ will be contained in different half-spaces.

Lemma 2 If $T(x, \sigma)$ is a cone complement, then there exists a hyperplane H such that $H \subset T(x, \sigma)$.

The generalised model in k-dimensions*

Before moving on to revealed preference analysis, it is necessary to generalise the descriptions of neutral zones in the two objectives case to that in the k objectives case.

As in the standard model, it is assumed that the indifference loci (i.e. the classes of iso-welfare points) are a set of parallel hyperplanes in the k-dimensional O-space. Formally, it is assumed that there exists $a \in E^k$ such that for any point $\bar{B}^i \in E^k$, the indifference class, $I(\bar{B}^i)$, may be described as follows: $I(\bar{B}^i) = \{x \mid x \in E^k \text{ and } x'a = \bar{B}^i a\} = H_a$. H_a is a hyperplane with normal a. We could think of these indifference hyperplanes as generated by the SWF, $W = a_1 B_1 + \ldots + a_k B_k$, as in the standard model.

In keeping with the Armstrong approach the government is allowed some imprecision in its preference. The neutral class or zone, as described earlier in this chapter, is generalised to the k-dimensional case and used to allow the government some room for imprecision. We assume that for any $\bar{B}^i \in E^k$, the neutral zone, $N(\bar{B}^i)$, is a displaced cone complement at $\bar{B}^i$. As before, the neutral zones at different points in E^k are assumed to be of the same shape. Formally, it is assumed that there exists $x \in E^k$ and a scalar $\sigma > 0$, such that for any $\bar{B}^i \in E^k$, $N(\bar{B}^i) = \{\bar{B}^i\} + T(x, \sigma) = T'(\bar{B}^i, x, \sigma)$ where $T(x, \sigma)$ is a cone complement.

Assumption 1 For all $\bar{B}^i \in E^k$, $I(\bar{B}^i) \subset N(\bar{B}^i)$.

The rationale behind this assumption is based on the Armstrong–Majumdar interpretation of neutrality and was discussed above. The existence of a hyperplane in $N(\bar{B}^i)$ is guaranteed by Lemma 2.

For $\bar{B}^i \in E^k$, if H_a is the indifference hyperplane and $T'(\bar{B}^i, x, \sigma)$ the neutral displaced cone complement, then the associated displaced cone contained in H_a^+, excluding $\bar{B}^i$, is called the *superior zone* to $\bar{B}^i$. Similarly the associated displaced cone contained in H_a^-, excluding $\bar{B}^i$, is called the *inferior zone* to $\bar{B}^i$. σ is called the *degree of precision*. An indifference hyperplane, along with the superior and inferior zones to $\bar{B}^i$ in E^3, is shown in Figure 3.10.

Note that $T(x, \sigma) = T(-x, \sigma)$. Hence, we could describe the same cone complement in terms of x or $-x$. We adopt the convention of choosing between these two so that if $T(y, \sigma)$ is a neutral zone, then $C(y, \sigma)$ is the superior zone and $-C(y, \sigma)$ the inferior one.

It is obvious that the larger the value of σ, the closer is the neutral zone to a hyperplane, and consequently the government's preference is more determinate or precise.

It is easily verified that our definition of neutral zones implies that neutrality is a symmetric relation and also that y lies in the inferior zone to x if and only if x is in the superior zone to y. As far as government preference goes, $\bar{B}^i$ is preferred to any point in the inferior zone to $\bar{B}^i$ and any point in the superior zone to $\bar{B}^i$ is preferred to $\bar{B}^i$. It will be assumed as before that if x is preferred to y, then given a choice between x and y, x will be chosen. The following assumption is now obvious.

Assumption 2 If $\bar{B}^j$ lies in the inferior zone to $\bar{B}^i$ then $\bar{B}^j$ will not be chosen if $\bar{B}^i$ is available. If $\bar{B}^j$ does not lie in the inferior zone to $\bar{B}^i$ then $\bar{B}^j$ may be chosen even if $\bar{B}^i$ is available.

We are now ready to face the problem of revealed preference. To apply

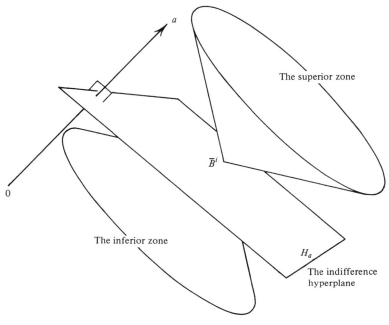

Figure 3.10

the generalised revealed preference technique, we have to first choose a
degree of precision. Let this be σ.[8] Once this is fixed, a cone complement
$T(x, \sigma)$ is a function of x, where $x \in E^k$. The aim of revealed preference
analysis is to discover the government's neutral zone. In other words, we
have to discover $x \in E^k$ such that $T(x, \sigma)$ is the government's neutral
zone (and, by extension, $C(x, \sigma)$ is the superior zone). As before, it will
seldom be possible to discover the precise x. So we merely attempt to
specify as small a subset of E^k as possible, within which the government's x
is expected to lie.

Unlike in the two-dimensional case, we focus our attention on the
government's neutral zones rather than its indifference hyperplanes.
It will be shown later that this method has the advantage of satisfying
the binary reconstruction property discussed above. Given that we are
trying to find the government's neutral zones, we can ignore indifference
hyperplanes. In fact, the government's preference could be such that there
exist no iso-welfare hyperplanes.

Assume that a government is observed to choose project p_1 from n
available projects: $p_1, p_2, \ldots, p_n$. For all i, p_i can be described by a k-ele-
ment vector $\bar{B}^i$. The *solution set* $\Omega_\sigma \subset E^k$ consists of those vectors x such

[8] σ must lie within certain limits such that for any $x \in E^k$, $C(x, \sigma)$ is a circular cone.

that the cone complement $T(x,\sigma)$ can be a neutral zone compatible with the government's choice. The next theorem follows directly from assumption 2 and the above observations.

Theorem 3*1 $x \in \Omega_\sigma$ (the solution set) if and only if, for all $i = 2, \ldots, n$, $\bar{B}^i \in [T(x,\sigma) \cup -C(x,\sigma)] + \{\bar{B}^1\}$ (i.e. $\bar{B}^2, \ldots, \bar{B}^n$ lie in the neutral or inferior zone to $\bar{B}^1$).

Let us confine ourselves, for the time being, to the case where the government chooses *one* project and rejects *one*. Let a government choose project p_1 and reject p_2, where p_1 and p_2 are characterised by $\bar{B}^1$ and $\bar{B}^2$ respectively ($\bar{B}^1, \bar{B}^2 \in E^k$). This act of choice is, from our point of view, the same as choosing $\bar{B}^1 - \bar{B}^1 = 0 = \bar{\bar{B}}^1$ (say) and rejecting $\bar{B}^2 - \bar{B}^1 = \bar{\bar{B}}^2$. This merely amounts to a shift of the origin as shown in Figure 3.11.

The solution set $\Omega_\sigma \subset E^k$ consists of vectors x such that $\bar{\bar{B}}^2 \in T(x,\sigma)$ or $\bar{\bar{B}}^2 \in -C(x,\sigma)$.

A solution set, being a collection of points within which the government's actual vector x lies, is more informative if it is small. Now, from the same observations of governmental choice, different solution sets may be evaluated by altering the degree of precision. The relation between different values of σ and the corresponding sets, Ω_σ, is a regular and an interesting one.

Theorem 3*2 If $\sigma < \psi$, then $\Omega_\psi \subset \Omega_\sigma$.

This theorem is proved in the appendix to this chapter, but an intuitive sketch may be provided here. A government has chosen 0 and rejected $\bar{\bar{B}}^2$. Consider the set of preferences consistent with this choice if no allowance is made for errors. Now, if a small allowance is made for errors obviously a larger set of preferences would be compatible. If this allowance for errors is further increased, the set of compatible preferences

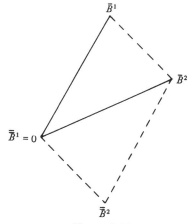

Figure 3.11

becomes larger as well. Now, σ and ψ are degrees of precision. Hence, $\sigma < \psi$ means that σ makes a greater allowance for errors than ψ. Hence, the set of preferences (compatible with the choice of 0 over $\bar{B}^2$) corresponding to σ is larger than that corresponding to ψ. I.e. $\Omega_\psi \subset \Omega_\sigma$.

It is therefore clear that if σ is made larger and larger starting from zero, then the solution sets will become smaller and smaller–each solution set being a subset of the preceding one. The extreme is reached when $\sigma = \sqrt{2}$. At this point the neutral zone collapses to a hyperplane. (This is proved in the next theorem). And we are back to the standard model. Given that an indifference class is a subset of the corresponding neutral class (assumption 1) and that both the indifference and neutral classes are hyperplanes, these two classes coincide, i.e. $I(x) = N(x)$ for all $x \in E^k$, as in the Lausanne approach. Hence the generalised model based on the Armstrong approach is a generalisation of the standard model founded on the Lausanne assumptions.

Theorem 3*3   The cone complement $T(x, \sqrt{2})$ is a hyperplane.

A rigorous proof is given in the appendix, but the intuition behind the theorem is easy to see. Consider two orthogonal (i.e. perpendicular)

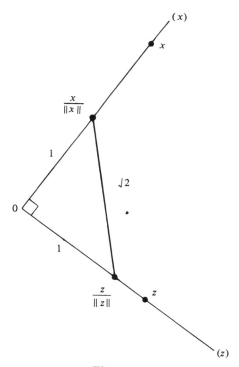

Figure 3.12

vectors, x and z in E^k. It is well known that this implies that $x'z = 0$. Hence, $[z, x] = \{2 - 2x'z/(\|z\| \|x\|)\}^{1/2} = \sqrt{2}$. This is also obvious by the Pythagoras theorem, since $[z, x]$ is the distance of the hypotenuse of a right-angled triangle with two sides of unit length, as shown in Figure 3.12.

Hence, the superior zone, $C(x, \sqrt{2})$, which contains all rays within a distance of $\sqrt{2}$ from ray (x), is a half space. Consequently, the inferior zone is a half-space as well. Discarding these zones, therefore, leaves us with a cone complement which is a hyperplane.

From Theorem 3*3, it is clear that the standard model and, hence, the Weisbrod and UNIDO models are a special case of the technique developed here. The solution set evaluated by the standard model is identical to that evaluated by the above method under the special assumption of the degree of precision being equal to $\sqrt{2}$.

Till now, we have confined ourselves to the case where the government chooses one project from an available pair. What happens if there are many pairs from each of which the government selects one project or if the government has a set containing more than two projects and it chooses one from it? How do we now evaluate the solution set? This is a simple task given that the present algorithm satisfies the binary reconstruction property. Let a government choose p_1 from $\{p_1, p_2, p_3\}$. Let $\bar{\Omega}$ be the solution set, i.e. for all $x \in \bar{\Omega}$, $T(x, \sigma)$ is a cone complement (and $C(x, \sigma)$ the superior zone) compatible with the choice of p_1 from $\{p_1, p_2, p_3\}$. Let the solution sets corresponding to the choices of p_1 from $\{p_1, p_2\}$ and $\{p_1, p_3\}$ be Ω^2 and Ω^3. If some $x \in \bar{\Omega}$, then obviously $x \in \Omega^2$ and $x \in \Omega^3$. If some $x \in \Omega^2 \cap \Omega^3$, then there exist a cone complement $T(x, \sigma)$ and a cone $-C(x, \sigma)$ at $p_1 \in E^k$ such that $p_2, p_3 \in T(x, \sigma) \cup -C(x, \sigma)$. This implies that $x \in \bar{\Omega}$. Hence, $\bar{\Omega} = \Omega^2 \cap \Omega^3$. A similar argument would have held if the government chose from n projects. Consequently, for calculating a general solution set we have to calculate solution sets for choices over pairs and then take their intersection.[9]

As far as the choice of the degree of precision goes, it is important to note that if σ is very high (i.e. close to $\sqrt{2}$), then there is the possibility that the government's actual degree of precision is lower and Ω_σ may be an empty set. On the other hand, as already mentioned in the 2-dimensional case, if σ is very small, then the solution set will be very large and consequently uninformative. Though it would be best if we could choose a degree of precision, σ, equal to the government's actual one, the inability to do so does not render the model useless. After all, by choosing a σ, all we are doing is allowing the government to be imprecise *up to* a certain degree. Certainly the government's imprecision can be *within* this limit.

---

[9] It is worth cautioning that if $x \in \bar{\Omega}$ and $T(x, \sigma)$ a possible neutral zone, then this does not imply that all hyperplanes $H \subset T(x, \sigma)$ are possible indifference classes.

If $\Omega_{\sqrt{2}} = \phi$, then it may be interesting to locate the critical σ at which Ω_σ changes from an empty set to a non-empty one. Let $\bar{\sigma}$ be such a critical degree of precision, which is defined as follows: $\bar{\sigma} = \sup_{\sigma \in \Delta} \sigma$, where $\Delta = \{\sigma | \Omega_\sigma \neq \phi\}$. We could think of $\bar{\sigma}$ as a degree of rationality. In the standard model if $\Omega_{\sqrt{2}} = \phi$, then the government was termed irrational. The idea of degrees of rationality could permit us to eschew this 0–1 concept of rationality used by Weisbrod and also in the standard model. This may, in some ways, be a more useful way of looking at the concept of rationality. An aesthetically better way of defining the degree of rationality is in terms of $\lambda = \bar{\sigma}/\sqrt{2}$, where $\bar{\sigma}$ is defined as above. The degree of rationality, λ, lies between 0 and 1. If $\lambda = 1$, then the agent is fully rational. If, however, $\lambda < 1$, then it does not mean that the government is irrational, as in the standard model, but merely that it is less than fully rational.

The generalised model developed in this chapter is designed to make allowance for certain types of limited indeterminateness in government preference. It was seen that this model could handle the sort of indeterminateness caused by perception problems of the kind discussed by Armstrong. It will be seen in Chapter 6 that the sort of incompleteness in government preference which stems from the government's ability to only 'partially' compare interpersonal utilities, as discussed by Sen (1970), may also be accommodated within our generalised model. The last section of this chapter discusses how a limited kind of interdepartmental conflict within the government may give rise to the type of neutral zones hypothesised here.

The problem of inter-departmental conflict

A government comprises many departments and it is quite possible that these departments have different preferences. Given that a government's preference is a combination of its departmental preferences, and that the balance of power between departments varies, we can no longer expect consistency from the government in areas where departments conflict. This multi-departmental feature of governments has received considerable attention in recent years in the theory of Multiple Objective Linear Programming (MOLP) (see Kornbluth, 1974). MOLP begins by assuming that each department has its own SWF. For example, let a government have two departments and let their indifference curves be L_1 and L_2 respectively as shown in Figure 3.2. Given a choice between x and y, y will be preferred to x, according to MOLP. This is quite reasonable, since y is preferred to x by both departments. However, given a choice between x and z in Figure 3.2, there is no definite answer, since departmental interests conflict here. In the framework of MOLP, it is then assumed that government preference between x and z is incomplete.

Arguing in the same way, the preference between x and any point in the shaded region at x is incomplete. In our terminology, the shaded region is the neutral class to x. Hence, MOLP suggests that neutral zones in two dimensions are representable by cone complements.

There are two important limitations to this approach. In the $k(k > 2)$ dimensional case, the neutral zone suggested by MOLP is no longer a cone complement. As long as the number of departments within government is finite, the superior zone is a convex polyhedral cone and not a circular cone. Nevertheless, given that precise department preferences are not known, cone complements may be used to set a maximum allowance for imprecision stemming from inter-departmental conflict.

The MOLP representation of intra-governmental conflict is of a very special kind and may fail to depict reality in many situations. There could be complex game-theoretic conflicts between departments which could render even the generalised model ineffective. Some of these are discussed in Chapter 7.

Appendix to Chapter 3

Lemma 1 If $H = \{x \mid x'a = 0\}$ is a bounding hyperplane for the circular cone C, then it must be a bounding hyperplane for $-C$. C and $-C$ will be contained in different half-spaces.

Proof Since H is a bounding hyperplane for C, we may assume without loss of generality that $y'a \geq 0$, for all $y \in C$. Now, let $z \in -C$. This implies $-z \in C$. Hence, $-z'a \geq 0$, which implies $z'a \leq 0$. Therefore H bounds $-C$. Note that $C \subset H^+$ and $-C \subset H^-$.

Lemma 2 If $T(x, \sigma)$ is a cone complement, then there exists a hyperplane H such that $H \subset T(x, \sigma)$.

Proof Let $C(x, \sigma)$ be one of the two circular cones associated with the cone complement $T(x, \sigma)$. Hence, it follows from the definition of a cone complement that $C(x, \sigma)$ is a convex cone and $C(x, \sigma) \neq E^k$. Hence, there exists a hyperplane, H, through the origin, which bounds $C(x, \sigma)$ (see Fenchel, 1953, p. 8, Corollary 1).

We now prove that $H \cap C(x, \sigma) = \{0\}$. First we prove $H \cap C(x, \sigma) \subset \{0\}$. Assume to the contrary that there exists z such that $z \neq 0$ and $z \in H \cap C(x, \sigma)$. Therefore, $z \in C(x, \sigma)$, which implies $[z, x] < \sigma$. Hence z lies in the interior of $C(x, \sigma)$. Consequently, $z \notin H$, which is a bounding hyperplane. But this is a contradiction. Hence, $H \cap C(x, \sigma) \subset \{0\}$. It is obvious that $\{0\} \subset H \cap C(x, \sigma)$. Therefore, $H \cap C(x, \sigma) = \{0\}$.

Since H bounds $C(x, \sigma)$, therefore, by Lemma 1, H bounds $-C(x, \sigma)$. By the same reasoning as above $\{0\} = H \cap -C(x, \sigma)$. This implies $H \setminus \{0\} \subset E^k \setminus \{C(x, \sigma) \cup -C(x, \sigma)\}$ which implies $H \subset \{E^k \setminus \{C(x, \sigma) \cup -C(x, \sigma)\}\} \cup \{0\} = T(x, \sigma)$.

Theorem 3*2 If $\sigma < \psi$, then $\Omega_\psi \subset \Omega_\sigma$.

Proof Without loss of generality, assume that the solution sets are evaluated from the government's act of choosing 0 and rejecting $\bar{\bar{B}}^2$. Let $x \in \Omega_\psi$. It follows from Theorem 3*1 that $\bar{\bar{B}}^2 \in T(x, \psi) \cup -C(x, \psi)$, which implies that $\bar{\bar{B}}^2 \notin C(x, \psi) \backslash \{0\}$. Now, $C(x, \sigma) \subset C(x, \psi)$, since $\sigma < \psi$. Hence, $\bar{\bar{B}}^2 \notin C(x, \sigma) \backslash \{0\}$. Therefore, by Theorem 3*1, $x \in \Omega_\sigma$. Hence, $\Omega_\psi \subset \Omega_\sigma$.

Theorem 3*3 The cone complement $T(x, \sqrt{2})$ is a hyperplane.

Proof Remember $T(x, \sqrt{2}) = \{E^k \backslash \{C(x, \sqrt{2}) \cup -C(x, \sqrt{2})\}\} \cup \{0\}$. It will be proved that $T(x, \sqrt{2}) = H = \{y \mid y'x = 0\}$. First we prove $T(x, \sqrt{2}) \subset H$. $z \in T(x, \sqrt{2}) \to z = 0$ or $z \in E^k \backslash \{C(x, \sqrt{2}) \cup -C(x, \sqrt{2})\}$. If $z = 0$, then $z \in H$. $z \in E^k \backslash \{C(x, \sqrt{2}) \cup -C(x, \sqrt{2})\} \to [z, x] \geq \sqrt{2}$, since $z \notin C(x, \sqrt{2})$, and $[-z, x] \geq \sqrt{2}$, since $z \notin -C(x, \sqrt{2})$.

$$\text{That implies } 2 - \frac{2z'x}{\|z\| \|x\|} \geq 2 \text{ and } 2 + \frac{2z'x}{\|z\| \|x\|} \geq 2.$$

$$\to \quad -z'x \geq 0 \text{ and } z'x \geq 0$$

$$\to \quad z'x = 0$$

$$\to \quad z \in H$$

The theorem is established by proving $H \subset T(x, \sqrt{2})$. Noting that $0 \in H$ and $0 \in T(x, \sqrt{2})$, all we have to prove is that $H \backslash \{0\} \subset T(x, \sqrt{2}) \backslash \{0\}$. $0 \neq z \in H \to z'x = 0$

$$\to \quad [z, x] = \left(2 - \frac{2z'x}{\|z\| \|x\|}\right)^{1/2} = \sqrt{2}$$

$$\to \quad z \notin C(x, \sqrt{2}) \cup -C(x, \sqrt{2})$$

$$\to \quad z \in T(x, \sqrt{2}).$$

4

A critique of rationality

Underlying both the standard and generalised models were assumptions of governmental rationality. We now pause to take a deeper look at these assumptions and at related questions which arise from them. But we begin elsewhere. Germinating from the works of Hicks and Samuelson, a vast literature has developed on revealed preference, choice functions and rationality. Arrow (1959), Richter (1966), Sen (1971) and Suzumura (1976), among many others, have worked to generalise and formalise these concepts. So we begin by elucidating this modern framework and the concept of rationality contained in it. In the light of this we review the rationality assumptions in our previous chapters. It will be argued that while the literature has provided elegance and generality to the theory of choice and rationality, it is not very useful in practical economics. This is followed by a discussion of the behaviouristic and other definitions of rationality. After this general discussion we move to the more mundane world of governments and their social welfare functions.

Choice functions and revealed preference

Samuelson (1938) started with the individual consumer who faced alternate *budget sets* (i.e. budget triangles in the two-good case) and chose a *single* element (i.e. a basket of commodities) from each set. Let us assume that these choices along with the corresponding budget sets are known. How do we decide whether or not the individual is rational? Samuelson suggested a simple consistency criterion, popularly known as the Weak Axiom of Revealed Preference, which states that 'if an individual selects batch one over batch two, he does not at the same time select batch two over batch one' (Samuelson, 1938, p. 65). This is a clear definition of rationality. Given any collection of budget sets and the corresponding choices, we could apply the axiom and determine whether the agent concerned is rational or not. If the axiom is violated anywhere, then the agent is irrational in the Samuelsonian sense.

Arrow (1959) set about relaxing the Samuelson framework in two major ways. He allowed for the possibility that budget sets need not be the only sets from which the agent chooses. This is a convenient step towards analysing government behaviour since governments frequently choose from collections other than budget sets (e.g. a set consisting of two alternatives: a bridge and a ferry service). Secondly, Arrow's consumer, unlike that of Samuelson, when faced with a set of alternatives, could have more than one 'best' element in it. Within this framework, which is retained by Richter (1966, 1971), Sen (1971) and Suzumura (1976), Arrow derives many interesting results, but we shall not dwell on them now. Instead, let us describe this framework in a more rigorous fashion as this is essential for some later comments.

Let X be the set of all alternatives and let K be a non-empty collection of non-empty subsets of X. For any S contained in K, $C(S)$ represents a 'choice set' or 'the chosen elements of S' (Sen, 1971, p. 307). In simple terms we could think of $C(S)$ – for the time being – as a set of the best elements in S. Now, C could be viewed as a function which for every $S \in K$ specifies a non-empty set $C(S) \subset S$ and it is called a *choice function* (Arrow, 1959). This is seen as a generalisation of the Samuelson framework in which X is a Euclidean space, K consists of only those subsets of X which are budget sets and $C(S)$ is a singleton.

Every agent has a choice function. Let us assume that an agent's choice function is known, i.e. we know the 'chosen elements' of the agent for every $S \in K$. Is this agent rational? This depends on how we define rationality. A simple definition, as discussed above, is that a choice function is rational if and only if it satisfies the Weak Axiom. The Weak Axiom – adapted to the Arrow–Sen framework – may be formally stated as follows: If for some $S \in K$, there exists $x, y \in S$ such that $x \in C(S)$ and $y \notin C(S)$, then there does not exist any $Z \in K$ such that $y \in C(Z)$ and $x \in Z$. There are many other definitions of rationality. For instance, a very weak notion of rationality is called *G-rationality* by Suzumura (1976) (see also Richter, 1971). But before considering this we need to define some terms formally.

A *preference relation* on X is a specification of preference between pairs of elements in X, i.e. it specifies for each pair of alternatives $x, y \in X$, whether x is at least as good as y, vice versa or neither.[1] This can be more rigorously stated. A preference relation R on X is a set consisting of only ordered pairs (x, y), where both x and y are elements of X (i.e. $R \subset X \times X$)[2]; and $(x, y) \in R$ implies that x is at least as good as y. For example, let $X = \{x, y, z\}$. Then $R = \{(x, y), (y, x), (y, z), (y, y), (z, x)\}$ is a preference relation.

---

[1] If neither x is at least as good as y, nor y at least as good as x, then we say that x and y are incomparable, or that the preference relation is incomplete over x and y. By an 'incomplete preference relation' we mean that there exists a pair of alternatives over which the preference relation is incomplete.

[2] In general, if R is a subset of the cartesian product $X \times X$, then R is called a *binary relation* on X. Hence a preference relation is a binary relation and so is the relation of neutrality N used in the previous chapter.

The fact that it reflects a rather peculiar preference does not deny its status as a preference relation. Of course, as we shall see later, rationality may require R to fulfil certain specifications. It is worth noting that $(x, y) \in R$ is at times expressed as xRy.

Given any preference relation, R, on X, the set of R-*greatest* elements of S (where $S \subset X$), denoted by $G(S, R)$ is defined as follows:

$$G(S, R) = \{x \mid x \in S \ \& \ \text{for all } y \in S, (x, y) \in R\}$$

In words, an x is an R-greatest element of S if and only if it is at least as good as each of the elements in S. In the example above, $G(X, R) = \{y\}$. Note that $x \notin G(X, R)$ since $(x, x) \notin R$.

Now we can define G-rationality. A choice function C (and, by extension, the agent possessing it) is called G-*rational* if and only if there exists a preference relation R on X such that for all $S \in K$, $C(S) = G(S, R)$. In other words, an agent is G-rational if a preference relation R, which explains his choices, is conceivable. It is possible that there exists more than one R which rationalises the agent's choices. Note that there are no requirements on the nature of R. Its existence is all we need. Hence, this is a very weak definition of rationality. This does not mean that no choice functions are G-irrational. We now illustrate these observations with examples.

Let $X = \{x, y, z\}$, $K = \{S_1, S_2\}$, $S_1 = \{x, y, z\}$ and $S_2 = \{x, y\}$. Consider the following choice function: $C(S_1) = \{x\}$ and $C(S_2) = \{x, y\}$. This is G-rational because we could construct $R = \{(x, x), (y, y), (x, y), (y, x), (x, z)\}$ which implies that $G(S_1, R) = C(S_1)$ and $G(S_2, R) = C(S_2)$. This is not the only possible rationalisation. $R' = R \cup \{(z, x)\}$ also rationalises the above choice function. Now, consider another choice function such that $C(S_1) = \{x\}$ and $C(S_2) = \{y\}$. This is not G-rational. Assume that there exists an R such that $G(S_1, R) = C(S_1)$ and $G(S_2, R) = C(S_2)$. By definition, $G(S_1, R) = \{x\}$ implies that $(x, y) \in R$ and $(x, x) \in R$. Hence, $x \in G(S_2, R)$. This contradiction establishes that no preference relation can rationalise the choice function. Similar examples are discussed by Richter (1971) and Suzumura (1976).

The non-uniqueness of rationalisation is an important property in the context of revealed preference analysis. It shows that two persons with identical choice functions could be guided by different motivations.

Stronger definitions of rationality may be obtained by not only requiring the *existence* of a preference relation which is compatible with the choices, but by requiring the relation to satisfy certain conditions.[3] For instance we could demand that R be complete (see p. 48, n.1), reflexive and

---

[3] It is worth noting though, that the mere *existence* of a relation R, compatible with a choice function, automatically implies that R will satisfy some weak conditions, especially if certain prior assumptions are granted (Mukherji, 1977). To obtain stronger rationality definitions we need to impose conditions on R which are stricter than these weak ones.

transitive.[4] Such a choice function is called *regular rational* by Richter (1971). These definitions of rationality merely demand different kinds of internal consistency of choice. Traditional consumer theory, however, imposes the additional requirement that if x vector-dominates y (i.e. x has more of all goods than y) then $(x, y) \in R$. This is not required here and, in fact, X need not even be a vector space. Consequently these modern rationality definitions *seem* to be a considerable weakening of those in traditional theory. But we shall have more to say on this.

This modern approach stemmed from the need to demonstrate that the many different concepts of rationality that are used in economics have interesting logical interconnections (e.g. a choice function satisfying the weak axiom necessarily satisfies G-rationality). However, in the context of our work, and in fact in any applied analysis, there remain certain shortcomings which render this approach inapplicable.

One major trouble originates from the definition of $C(S)$. This definition is usually left vague, merely stating that $C(S)$ consists of 'the chosen elements of S' (Sen, 1971, p. 307) or that 'it represents those alternatives which are chosen from S' (Suzumura, 1976, p. 150). Clearly this cannot be the alternative *actually* chosen, because then $C(S)$ would contain a single element. Hence, the intended definition can be stated, based on Richter (1971) as follows: $C(S)$ is that subset of S from which the individual would choose when choosing a single element from S and between the elements of $C(S)$ he is indifferent as to which one he chooses. Whether we adopt exactly this definition or some similar one, it is obvious that $C(S)$ is not observable. When a consumer chooses a basket of goods, he does not reveal the other baskets which he would not have minded choosing. Now rationality assumptions in this modern framework are based on choice functions. So if we want to base our analysis on observed behaviour, we are stranded, since choice sets cannot be observed.

Some limited information regarding $C(S)$ can be obtained from observation. If an agent is observed to choose a single element from S, then we can be sure that this chosen element, by definition, lies in $C(S)$. We need a new name for this *actually* chosen element. Let $T(S)$ be the set consisting of the element actually chosen from S. We shall refer to $T(S)$ as the *selected set*. T could be viewed as a function which for every $S \in K$ specifies a singleton set $T(S) \subset S$ and we call it a *selection function*. A selection function is observable and could be used as a basis for rationality definitions.

The concept of G-rationality may be adapted to fit this new information base. *Potential G-rationality* – as we shall call it here – requires that there exists a relation R such that the selected element is one of the best available elements. Formally, a selection function is potentially G-rational

---

[4] An R is reflexive if, for all $x \in X$, $(x, x) \in R$, i.e. each x is at least as good as itself, and it is transitive if, for all $x, y, z \in X$, $(x, y) \in R$ and $(y, z) \in R$ implies that $(x, z) \in R$.

if and only if there exists a preference relation R on X and a choice function C on K such that for all $S \in K$, $T(S) \subset C(S) = G(S, R)$. Given that $G(S, R)$ is non-empty, for all $S \in K$, there exists a choice function C, such that $C(S) = G(S, R)$. Hence, potential G-rationality merely demands that there exists R on X such that for all $S \in K$, $T(S) \subset G(S, R)$. But it is easily seen that this condition is fulfilled by all selection functions. Let T be any selection function on K. Define R to be such that for all $x, y \in X, (x, y) \in R$. In other words, the agent is indifferent over all pairs. Then $G(S, R) = S$ for all $S \in K$. Hence, $T(S) \subset G(S, R)$, for all $S \in K$. So all selection functions are potentially G-rational. Not only that, since the R described above is complete, reflexive and transitive, it is obvious that all selection functions are potentially regular rational. An agent cannot but be rational!

G-rationality was always a very weak requirement but by altering it for practical application, it has become impossible to demonstrate G-irrationality. Now, let us look back at the traditional theory. There, rationality was based, not on choice functions, but on selection functions. Not distinguishing between these does not cause many problems in the case of Samuelson's work since he assumed strong ordering which means that $C(S)$ is a singleton and is identical to $T(S)$. But not so with Hicks (1956). When, in the modern framework, $C(S)$ was permitted to contain more than one element, this was no generalisation of Hicks, who never denied this possibility. Hicks was dealing with $T(S)$ which is, by definition, a singleton. Moreover, in this framework it is quite useless to use weak rationality notions like G-rationality since all agents would then be rational. The set of alternatives, X, that Hicks was concerned with, comprised a vector space; and he demanded that the R underlying an agent's behaviour be such that if x vector-dominates y, then $(x, y) \in R$ and $(y, x) \notin R$. Clearly, some such assumption is essential for having a useful definition of rationality. Modern concepts like G-rationality require that either our theory be based on non-observables or that it be so adapted that all behaviour is rational.

In the Weisbrod and standard models, an even stronger requirement was placed on R. As in Hicks, R was supposed to subsume vector dominance, and it was further assumed that R be such as to permit the existence of a linear SWF.

In terms of the framework developed above, we can now succinctly summarise the rationality concepts used in the models for evaluating government preferences which we have discussed in the earlier chapters. In the standard model, K consisted of finite subsets of E^k (though not necessarily all finite subsets). A government with a selection function T was called rational if and only if there existed on E^k a linear function $W(\bar{B}) = \bar{a}\,\bar{B}$, where $\bar{B} \in X$ and $\bar{a} > 0$, such that for all $S \in K$, $W(T(S)) \geq W(y)$, for all $y \in S$. In the generalised model, rationality was no longer treated as a 0–1 concept. A government which satisfied the rationality condition of the standard model was termed fully rational. But not satisfying this condition did not necessarily make the government irrational. The government could still be partially rational.

The Arrow–Sen analysis also suggests ways of generating preference relations from choice functions, which may be interesting to the revealed preference analyst. One suggested method is to define a relation R^* such that $(x, y) \in R^*$ whenever $x \in C(S)$ and $y \in S$ for some $S \in K$.[5] To *apply* this method we would have to replace the use of choice functions by selection functions. However, this approach has severe shortcomings. If the set of alternatives, X, is an infinite set and the choices are faced in finite bundles (i.e. for all $S \in K$, S is a finite set) then this method will not reveal any preference over a substantial area of the alternatives in X. In the context of the basic model where $X(=E^k)$ was an infinite set and every $S \in K$ was assumed to be finite, this method of preference revelation would not take us very far. If, on the other hand, we assume, as in Chapter 2, that there exists a linear SWF which the government maximises, then every act of choice by the government reveals a quasi-ordering (i.e. a relation which is transitive and reflexive) over the entire local O-space, E^k. This revealed relation is complete over a large number of ordered pairs in E^k.

In Figure 4.1 let the government select p_1 from the set $\{p_1, p_2\}$. In terms of R^*, this act reveals nothing more than $p_1 R^* p_2$. However, in terms of the basic model, this act reveals that the government's indifference curve lies somewhere in between lines α and β. This in turn reveals a

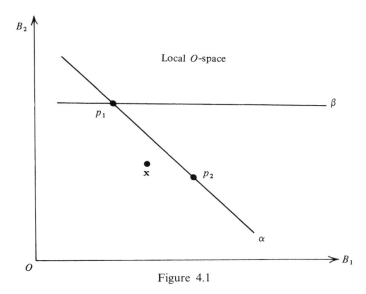

Figure 4.1

[5] A further preference relation is generated by taking the 'transitive closure' of R^*.

quasi-ordering over the entire local O-space. For example, we now know that the government prefers p_1 to x, which lies below the line α.

The assumptions (like the *linear* SWF) that had to be made to get this extra mileage were very strong compared to the assumptions made in the Arrow–Sen–Suzumura framework. The generalised model allows for assumptions which lie between these two extremes.

On definitions of rationality

We have just encountered various kinds of rationality concepts. They are all defined in terms of choice functions or selection functions. Let us recapitulate and see what is the essence of these definitions.

It should be remembered that a selection function T specifies for each set $S \in K$, a singleton set $T(S)$ which consists of that element in S which the agent actually chooses. Let F be the set of all selection functions. A *definition of rationality* specifies a set $Q \subset F$ such that an agent is rational if and only if his selection function T is an element of Q. If Q and Q' are two definitions of rationality and $Q \subset Q'$, and $Q' \not\subset Q$, then Q is a stronger definition of rationality. One extreme definition of rationality is to specify Q to be a unit set. 'My way is the only rational way' implies such an extreme definition. The other extreme is to define $Q = F$. According to this definition all behaviour is rational. The concepts of potential G-rationality and regular-rationality fall into this category. Also, if we believe that human beings always maximise happiness and then define rationality as a happiness maximising choice,[6] then again we are implying $Q = F$. For a definition to be useful in economic theory, it must lie well within the above extremes. The stronger the definition of rationality used in a theory, the more informative will the theory be. However, the possibility of the theory being empirically contradicted will also be high.

One common feature of all these rationality definitions, no matter how strong or weak, is that they are behaviouristic definitions. If the behaviour of two agents is identical, then these definitions will never say that only one of them is rational.

It would be erroneous to think that all concepts of rationality could be reduced to a form which fits into this framework. There could be important non-behaviouristic concepts of rationality in which the same overt action by two individuals could lead to one being branded as rational and the other irrational. In fact we often use such concepts of rationality in everyday life. Consider a game of chess in which there is a move, m, which is a sure winner if backed up by a particular move, ten moves later; but otherwise it is a very foolish move. If an amateur makes

---

[6] This is what the Austrian economists were doing. They simultaneously held 'that people acted to maximize their utility' and 'that however people behaved, they would presumably not have done so unless it maximised their satisfaction' (Samuelson, 1972, p. 255).

move *m*, then he may be termed irrational, though the same move made by Morphy would not lead Morphy to be termed so. What is more important is that even if this individual discovers the specific back-up move in the course of the game and turns out a winner so that his game is no different from that of a grandmaster's, his move, *m*, may still be called irrational. Our commonsensical notion of rationality very often does have a non-behaviouristic facet like this. If we accept a definition of rationality which does take into account the reason behind an action, and there may be good reason to do so, then we cannot brand a government rational or irrational merely by observing its behaviour.

Governmental rationality

It has been pointed out above that in the standard model a government was called rational if it had a selection function *T* such that it permitted the existence of a linear SWF. This was criticised as a very strong definition and it was relaxed in the generalised model. We have just noted that there can be an even more fundamental criticism on the grounds that this rationality concept is based purely on behaviour and this may be inadequate. It provides no insight into the motivation of the choices. The chess player, who foolishly makes a brilliant move, is – in behaviouristic terms – as rational as Morphy. This possibility of different mental states leading to identical behaviour is a serious problem for the revealed preference analyst who is trying to say something about the mental states.

This is better understood with the aid of an extreme example. Consider a mono-coloured object. When different human beings view this object, the colour they see may be quite different, even though they may call it by the same name, e.g. red or blue. There is, in general, no reason to believe that the perception of colour of different human beings is the same. It is quite possible that what I see as red, you see as my black, and what I see as black, you see as my red, and the former we both call red and the latter black.[7] Our behaviour does not reveal that we perceive colours differently. When the red light at the traffic crossing flashes we both brake, for we know that this colour, called red, means stop. The fact that it looks red to me and my black to you does not in any way affect our behaviour. We are not called colour blind because we can distinguish all colours. Your behaviour could have been predicted by assuming that your perception of colours is the same as mine.

This possibility of different mental states manifesting the same behaviour is at the same time a matter for joy for the positive theorist only interested in predicting behaviour, and a misfortune for the revealed preference analyst. For the former this implies that, when describing an

---

[7] While for the philosophically minded there may be cause to quiz over the 'meaning' of this 'proposition', we refrain, here, from such profundity.

agent's behaviour by assuming that some function guides him, we may be wrong in the sense that there may be a different mechanism guiding him, but we could still be predicting his behaviour accurately. However, if our purpose is to *reveal* preferences then this very fact, that different mental mechanisms could manifest the same overt action, is a serious drawback. The fact that a government's behaviour is such that it can be explained by assuming that a particular SWF guides it, may not be of any significance.

What does all this indicate in terms of evaluating government preference? It clearly points to the danger of deciding on a government's rationality in making a set of choices on the basis of nothing other than just that set of choices. We have to have information on the government's past choices and its socio-political environment, just as one way to determine whether an individual makes a brilliant chess move coincidentally or cleverly is to get further information as to whether he has a good record as a chess player or not, whether he is calculating or rash, etc. Of course, some problems, like the colour problem discussed above, would not be solvable by this method. But this does not alter the fact that for a judgement on a particular behaviour, the analyst should not confine himself to a study of *that* behaviour only. To understand a government's economic choice it may be necessary to enquire into its political character, for the same choice could be a consequence of quite different motives.

There are many other difficulties involved in judging the rationality of governments. We discuss two of them here. The first difficulty concerns the possibility of transient preferences and the second stems from the fact that some choices are, in fact, combinations of short-run choices.

SWFs of governments can change over time. But it is important to note that a change in an SWF could be of two types: (1) The GWF remains constant but the LWF changes as a result of the economy shifting its position in the objective space.[8] (2) The GWF changes. The Weisbrod (1968) model runs into difficulty whether (1) or (2) holds. As far as the standard model is concerned, (1) creates no problems, since data from different localities are treated separately. However, (2) would cause difficulties and might render combined solution sets meaningless.

A seeming change in government preference could be caused by the 'learning process'. This is caused by the fact that a government seldom faces the same choice vector repeatedly. Hence, it is liable to make mistakes and alter its behaviour as it learns more. Kornai (1971) writes: 'governments generally do learn; they learn from their historical experience and they modify their policies accordingly'. This problem is, at least in principle, surmountable.

Let the government have n projects from which it has to choose one.

---

[8] The terms GWF and LWF are discussed in Chapter 2.

From each project p_i, the government expects a certain vector of benefits, $\bar{B}^i$. And from each $\bar{B}^i$ it expects a certain amount of welfare, W^i. Two possible sources of errors in project choice are the following.

(a) The realised $\bar{B}^i$ diverges from the expected $\bar{B}^i$.

(b) The realised W^i diverges from the expected W^i.[9]

Errors usually occur because of unfamiliarity with the alternatives of choice. A government has to choose from widely differing sets of projects, and to gain familiarity here is difficult. However, since every p_i plots into the O-space, the government gets practice in choosing between different combinations of the same k objectives. Therefore, the government is not unfamiliar with translating $\bar{B}^i$ to W^i, though it may be unfamiliar with translating p_i to $\bar{B}^i$. This means that errors in choice are perhaps more likely to be caused by (a). If this be so then most problems are solved by using for data the $\bar{B}^i$ *expected by the government* from p_i, and not the actual $\bar{B}^i$, for all i.

An example

A government facing a choice between p_1 and p_2 calculates that p_1 is expected to generate the following vector of benefits: $[100, 50]$, i.e. 100 units of B_1 and 50 units of B_2. Similarly, p_2 is expected to generate $[120, 40]$. The government says that it (strongly) prefers p_1 to p_2. The project is implemented and realisation belies expectation as p_1 actually generates $[130, 30]$. The next year the government faces the same choice and this time it prefers p_2 to p_1. Clearly the preference in the set X is inconsistent, because p_1 is preferred to p_2 and p_2 is preferred to p_1. But let us see what preference has been expressed in the O-space. First, $[100, 50]$ was preferred to $[120, 40]$; and the following year $[120, 40]$ was preferred to $[130, 30]$. There is no inconsistency in this.

A different problem stems from the fact that what is feasible in the future may depend on what is chosen in the present. This makes it possible for a government to take a series of optimal decisions in the short run and land up with a sub-optimal long-run alternative. This could occur even when the SWF is unchanged. A simple example illustrates this. Let a government be faced with the choice of transforming its economy into states x or y in five years. In a further five years, the economy can be transformed into social states x_1 or x_2 from x and y_1 or y_2 from y. Let the government's preference over x_1, x_2, y_1 and y_2 be in that order, and let it prefer y to x. Now if the government was involved in planning for five years at a time it would first choose y and then choose y_1. If a revealed preference analyst, studying this economy ten years later argues that ten years ago the government could have planned for x_1, x_2, y_1 and y_2

---

[9] A similar distinction, in a different context, has been discussed by Majumdar (1958), p. 113.

and it chose y_1 and therefore revealed a preference of y_1 over the rest, he will clearly be wrong. The error occurs because the choice of y_1 was not a direct one, i.e. it was not chosen directly from the set $\{x_1, x_2, y_1, y_2\}$. It was the consequence of two optimal choices. If the government had planned directly for ten years it would have chosen x_1 instead of y_1. Hence, a revealed preference judgement should be used only for direct choices.

The nature of government

The concept of rationality belongs to the domain of individuals or agents. Hence, to discuss the rationality of a government is to implicitly accept that a government can be considered to be an agent. But can a government really be treated as an agent in the sense in which, say, Debreu (1959) speaks of economic agents?

The concept of an agent or an individual is defined succinctly by Luce and Raiffa (1957). The term individual is not used in a 'biological–social' sense but in a 'functional' one:

'Any decision-maker – a single human being or an organisation – which can be thought of as having a unitary interest motivating its decisions can be treated as an individual' (p. 13).

Taking note of the Luce and Raiffa definition, it is clear that the mere fact that a government is not one human being does not rule out the possibility of it being treated as an individual or an agent. What is questionable is whether it can be said in any sense that a government has 'a unitary interest motivating its decisions'. The most casual empiricism makes it difficult to answer this in the affirmative. It has already been pointed out, and is trivially obvious, that a government is a complex organisation, consisting of various departments which often have widely divergent aims. Its leadership is not permanent. Even when there is no overt change in leadership, there are shifts in the balance of power which may alter the government's motivation. This casts considerable doubt on the validity of the assumption that a government is an *agent*. An example of the sort of error which may be committed by ignoring the group character of a government and by treating it as an agent is discussed in Chapter 7. Also, once the government is recognised as having a multiplicity of aims and various departments and wings, it becomes difficult to *identify* the government. In an idealised situation there is a clear set of policy-makers who take the ultimate decisions based on the evaluations done by project formulators and evaluators. These policy-makers comprise the government. In reality, it is difficult to say who makes the policies. The ministers may take the final decision but they are influenced by interest groups and lobbies. Once the nebulous structure of governments is recognised, doubts arise about the meaningfulness of talking about governmental preference and rationality, or the lack of it. Some problems of interest groups are looked into in Chapter 8.

In closing, it ought to be pointed out that the assumption that an individual human being can be treated as an agent may also be questioned. A human being often has conflicting aims (Meade, 1974). After all, an individual human being's mind also has its departments – values, tastes, etc. (Harsanyi, 1955; Pattanaik, 1968).

5

Welfare maximisation and evaluation cost

A fundamental premise on which most theories of revealed preference are based is that, given a choice, an agent selects the alternative which yields the greatest welfare. This assumption may be valid if there is no cost involved in evaluating the welfares of different alternatives. But if the evaluation cost happens to be positive then this assumption loses its rationale.[1] Then, even though an agent may continue to maximise welfare, this may no longer imply selecting the alternative which gives maximum welfare. This creates immense problems for the revealed preference analyst. The next section discusses this.

The presence of a positive evaluation cost could cause problems, more momentous than merely thwarting the efforts of the revealed preference analyst. It could make it impossible for a decision-maker to maximise welfare in any meaningful sense. This is explained in greater detail later.

Project choice and evaluation cost

In most revealed preference approaches it is assumed that an agent chooses an alternative x only if $W(x) \geq W(y)$, for all feasible alternatives y. This is supposed to follow directly from the more basic assumption that economic agents maximise welfare.[2] If the cost of evaluating the alternative is zero then these assumptions may be reasonable. But if the cost of evaluation is positive then the arrow of implication from the latter basic assumption to the former is snapped.

Let us state this more formally and in terms of government behaviour. Consider statements α and β:

α : Government maximises welfare.

---

[1] Scitovsky (1976) refers to a similar issue rather eloquently: 'The Economist's traditional picture of the economy resembles nothing as much as a Chinese restaurant with its long menu. Customers choose from what is on the menu and are assumed always to have chosen what most pleases them. That assumption is unrealistic, not only of the economy, but of Chinese restaurants' (p. 149). For a discussion of this assumption in the context of merit wants see Basu (1976).

[2] In the context of risky situations, the term 'welfare' should be interpreted as *expected* welfare', and, consequently, welfare maximising behaviour should be interpreted as expected welfare maximising behaviour.

β : When choosing from a set of projects, a government will choose one with maximum welfare.

What we try to argue here is that α implies β only in the absence of evaluation costs. Many models of revealed preference assume β as a consequence of the more fundamental assumption α. The presence of evaluation costs weakens the basis of these models.

Before proceeding further, we need to define some terms. *Evaluation* is the activity of locating an alternative with maximum welfare from a set of alternatives. *Evaluation cost* then refers to the cost involved in this activity. An *evaluated choice* is a choice made after locating an optimal alternative, i.e. after evaluation. In order to keep the analysis simple we shall assume that there are two alternatives from which the agent chooses one. This choice, it will be assumed, can be made in two ways. It can be an evaluated choice or an unevaluated one. The concept of degrees of evaluation, where the better the evaluation the greater the possibility of locating the optimal alternative or project, will not be dealt with here. Here, an evaluated choice certainly leads to the superior alternative and an unevaluated choice would imply that there are no reasons to believe that the chosen alternative is or is not the superior one.

An unevaluated choice can be made in various ways. The agent could just grab one alternative. He could go by some superstition. We shall assume that he makes an equi-probable choice between the two alternatives. For example, he could toss a coin to decide which alternative he will pick. This sort of unevaluated choice will be called an *unappraised choice*. Hence, in our framework, given a choice between A and B, the government can make either an evaluated choice or an unappraised one. Most of the above simplifying assumptions need not worry us. This chapter discusses the problems of optimal choice, given evaluation costs. A more complex model is likely to strengthen the conclusions of this chapter rather than weaken them.

If a decision-maker is familiar with the alternatives facing him (e.g. an apple and an orange), then the evaluation cost (i.e. the cost of locating the optimal alternative) is zero and it seems reasonable to expect him to make an evaluated choice. However, most choices – especially the choices of projects by governments – involve considerable evaluation costs. In such a case there is no *a priori* reason to expect the decision-maker to make an evaluated choice. In fact, the motive of welfare maximisation itself may then prompt an unappraised choice. These ideas are easily formalised.

Let there be two projects A and B. Let the cost of evaluating A and B be C_1. We assume that C_1 is given in the same units as welfares from A and B, i.e. $W(A)$ and $W(B)$. If the government makes an evaluated choice then it can be sure of choosing the optimal project. Hence, denoting the act of an evaluated choice by E_1, we get

$$W(E_1) = \max \{W(A), W(B)\} - C_1$$

An unappraised choice, on the other hand, is costless and it involves an equal probability of selecting A or B. Consequently, if the act of an unappraised choice between A and B is denoted by D_1, then

$$W(D_1) = \tfrac{1}{2} W(A) + \tfrac{1}{2} W(B)$$

The government will make an evaluated choice if and only if

$$W(E_1) \geq W(D_1)^3$$

That is $W(E_1) - W(D_1) = [\max \{W(A), W(B)\} - C_1] - [\tfrac{1}{2} W(A) + \tfrac{1}{2} W(B)]$

$$\begin{aligned} &= \tfrac{1}{2} | W(A) - W(B)| - C_1 \\ &= \tfrac{1}{2} X - C_1 \geq 0 \end{aligned} \tag{5.1}$$

where $X = | W(A) - W(B)|^4$

If the inequality in (5.1) does not hold then the government makes an unappraised choice. If $C_1 = 0$, then (5.1) holds. But if $C_1 > 0$ then there is no *a priori* reason to believe either that (5.1) holds or does not hold. This corroborates what was intuitively stated above.

In the context of revealed preference theory, Sen (1973a) said, in his inaugural lecture, 'I am not totally persuaded that you in fact did choose the particular chair you have chosen through a careful evaluation of the pros and cons of sitting in each possible chair that was vacant when you came in'. What we have argued is that if 'a careful evaluation' of chairs has a high cost, and the difference between the comforts of the best and worst chairs not large, then Sen may well be right, but not because the audience was not maximising welfare, but rather because it was maximising welfare in a deeper sense, i.e. it was satisfying α but not β (of course, interpreting α and β in terms of individuals rather than governments).

Of course, α may not be satisfied either. In fact, it will be argued that given some very plausible conditions, the presence of evaluation costs may imply that an agent cannot be said to maximise welfare in any meaningful sense. As a stepping stone to this problem, consider the following example.

An example

Let $W(A) = 100$, $W(B) = 90$ and $C_1 = 20$. Should the government make an evaluated or an unappraised choice between A and B?

---

[3] In reality, if $W(E_1) = W(D_1)$, then the government will be indifferent between choosing E_1 and D_1. But for the sake of simplicity we have assumed that the government will select E_1.
[4] For any real number $y, |y| = \max \{y, -y\}$.

It is easy to check that $W(E_1) - W(D_1) = \frac{1}{2}.10 - 20 = -15$. Consequently the government *should* make an unappraised choice.

The interesting question in the above example is whether the government *will* make an unappraised choice or not. Clearly, *if* the government knows that $|W(A) - W(B)| = 10$ and that $C_1 = 20$, then it will immediately see that (5.1) is violated and it will make an unappraised choice. But how reasonable is it to assume that the government knows the value of $|W(A) - W(B)|$ and C_1? Since $C_1 > 0$ it is clear that the government does not know (i.e. prior to evaluation) the values of $W(A)$ and $W(B)$. In that case it seems not unnatural to assume that it does not know the value of $|W(A) - W(B)|$. Hence, it is unlikely that government will know the values of $W(E_1)$ and $W(D_1)$.

Hence, if the government wants to make a welfare maximising choice between E_1 and D_1 then it has to *evaluate* E_1 and D_1 first. Let the act of an evaluated choice between E_1 and D_1 (i.e. whether to make an evaluated or an unappraised choice from A and B) be denoted by E_2. Let the cost of this evaluation be C_2. If $C_1 > 0$, then it seems natural to assume $C_2 > 0$ (in fact usually C_2 will be $> C_1$) because in order to evaluate E_1 and D_1 (i.e. to calculate whether (5.1) is true or false) one would usually have to evaluate $W(A)$ and $W(B)$, and more. Let the act of making an unappraised choice between E_1 and D_1 be denoted by D_2. Using arguments similar to that used above, we get

$$W(E_2) = \max \{W(E_1), W(D_1)\} - C_2 \qquad (5.2)$$
and $\qquad W(D_2) = \frac{1}{2} W(E_1) + \frac{1}{2} W(D_1)$

Given $C_2 > 0$ there is no way of knowing *a priori* whether $W(E_2) \geq W(D_2)$ or $W(E_2) < W(D_2)$.[5]

In order to make a welfare maximising choice between E_2 and D_2, again the government has to evaluate and this will again involve some costs. And so on. It is clear that this chain is endless. Hence, the government will at some stage have to make a decision based on faith. Consequently, we cannot say in any meaningful way that the government maximises welfare.

By modifying some of the assumptions made above and by broadening the framework of analysis adopted in this chapter, more interesting

---

[5] It may be argued that (5.2) is an inaccurate description because in the process of incurring C_2 (i.e. while evaluating E_1 and D_1) A and B get automatically evaluated. Hence,

$$W(E_2) = \max \{\max \{W(A), W(B)\}, W(D_1)\} - C_2$$
$$= \max \{W(A), W(B)\} - C_2$$

Clearly this is different from (5.2), which implies

$$W(E_2) = \max \{\max \{W(A), W(B)\} - C_1, W(D_1)\} - C_2$$

However, even with this alteration, our main conclusion (which states that it is not known *a priori* whether E_2 or D_2 is preferable) remains unaffected.

results may be obtained. Our purpose was merely to demonstrate some of the problems caused by evaluation costs in the theory of revealed preference. For this the above simple analysis is sufficient.

We have argued that given positive evaluation costs, β – a basic assumption in most revealed preference theories – does not follow from α, and given some plausible conditions, α itself ceases to be an appropriate assumption.

Graaff's conjecture and revealed preference

It has been argued by Graaff (1975) that β is likely to hold for large projects. Graaff writes, 'cost–benefit analysis is itself costly, both because it is time-consuming and because of the skills it requires. For this reason it is likely to be confined to big projects.' This means that whereas choices from among small projects may be made without evaluation, choices from among big projects are made after evaluation. If this argument is valid then we could analyse government preferences but would have to base our analysis on the government's choice of large projects only.

Let us first examine Graaff's conjecture more closely. Assume that a government, though ignorant about $W(A)$ and $W(B)$, knows the difference between the two, i.e. $|W(A) - W(B)| = X$; and it also knows C_1. In order to be more realistic, we may assume that the government has an expectation of X and C_1, rather than a knowledge of their precise values. This can easily be accommodated in the ensuing discussion but we shall refrain from doing so for the sake of simplicity.

It has been shown that the government would evaluate and choose rather than make an unappraised choice if and only if (5.1) holds. Now, it is usually true that if the projects in question are big ones, then the welfare gap, X, between the two projects will be large as well. The welfare difference between an apple and an orange will *usually* be less than that between a thermal power station and a hydro-electric one. If S is the average size of projects A and B, then the above statement may be embodied in the following assumption:

(A1) As S becomes larger, so does X.

Graaff's conjecture seems to be based on (A1). The larger the S, the larger the value of X and consequently, the greater the likelihood of (5.1) being satisfied and E_1 being chosen.

But, now, a little reflection shows that if we accept (A1), we should accept another similar assumption:

(A2) As S becomes larger, so does C_1.

Not only is the welfare gap between an apple and an orange smaller than that between thermal and hydro-electric power stations, but so is the cost of evaluating the former two compared to that of the latter two.

Given (A2), it is no longer possible to assert, without qualification, that $\frac{1}{2}X - C_1$ is larger for larger projects. It all depends on the responsiveness of C_1 and X to project size.

Remarks on some standard models

In the light of the above discussion, a look is taken at some standard approaches of evaluating government preferences. In the UNIDO analysis the onus of evaluating project benefits lies on the revealed preference analyst. He is supposed to present the benefit vectors of all projects to the government, and the government merely chooses the best project. It seems likely that once the benefit vectors are calculated, there is no cost involved in finding the best project, though this may be questioned. Given this, as far as the government is concerned, there is no evaluation cost and consequently, if α is granted, then β follows directly.

In the approaches of Weisbrod (1968) and Mera (1969) there is no guarantee that β is satisfied. In these models the chosen project could well have been an unevaluated choice.[6] Hence, the usefulness of the governmental weights revealed by these models may be open to doubt.

It has been argued above that if project evaluation is costly then (i) α may not imply β and (ii) it is likely that α itself may not hold. This, nevertheless, does not negate the possibility of β being true. β may still hold, though not as a consequence of α. And fortunately, when β is satisfied, it will usually be obvious, as an evaluation process is generally accompanied by the formation of planning bodies and blueprints. Once it is ascertained that a choice is an evaluated one, revealed preference techniques may be applied.

---

[6] In the case of Mera, a project should be interpreted as a tax scheme.

6

The measurement of utility and interpersonal aggregation

The concept of an SWF has been widely used in the preceding chapters. Different SWFs entail different assumptions regarding the measurability and interpersonal comparability of utility. Hence, if a government decides to base its decisions on a particular SWF, it is tacitly accepting some measurability and comparability assumptions, i.e. a particular informational base. For example, a government cannot use an 'equity conscious' SWF if interpersonal utilities are not 'level comparable'. This chapter examines the axiomatic structure of relationships between different concepts of measurability and comparability and different types of SWFs. Such an examination is important as it reveals which assumptions of measurability and comparability are compatible and which are not.

This also raises the interesting question as to what happens to government preferences if the required informational assumptions are not fully met. We elucidate the concept of 'partial interpersonal comparisons' and then study the nature of social indifference curves which would arise from the government's ability to compare interpersonal utilities only partially. It is demonstrated that this causes the sort of indeterminateness in governmental preferences which was described in Chapter 3.

The measurement of utility: quasi-cardinality

Most discussions regarding the measurement of utility have – with notable exceptions (Little, 1950; Seigel, 1956; Fishburn, 1964; Sen, 1970a; Fine, 1974; Blackorby, 1975) – centred around cardinality and ordinality. In the context of demand theory under certainty or in applying various equity notions, like the Weak Equity Axiom of Sen (1973) or Hammond's (1977) Equity Axiom, utility has been assumed to be ordinal. It will be argued later that in the latter case this assumption may not be necessary. On the other hand, when the purpose has been to explain behaviour under uncertainty, as analysed by von Neumann & Morgenstern (1944) or Friedman & Savage (1948) then cardinality has been regarded as the appropriate scale.

Steeped in conventional theory, many economists find it difficult to accept that any utility measure can exist *between* ordinality and cardinality.

But the range between ordinality and cardinality is spanned by a whole set of quasi-cardinal scales. When ordinality has been found weak, frequently a jump has been taken to cardinality, but this is not necessary. The suggestion that 'roughly' cardinal scales be used was made much earlier by Little (1950, p. 37). Before describing quasi-cardinality let us be clear about ordinal and cardinal utilities.

Let X be the set of alternative social states. An individual has a set L of real-valued utility functions defined over X. A utility function is denoted by U, ϕ or ψ, i.e. $L = \{U, \phi, \psi, \ldots\}$. A single utility function is not, in itself, meaningful. An individual's preference is expressed in terms of L, the set of permitted utility functions. A particular preference relation is supposed to hold if and only if it is implied by all $U \in L$. The extent of measurability of utility depends on the definition of L.

For notational economy we need to introduce some short forms. For $x, y, a, b \in X$, $U_x = U(x), \Delta U_{xy} = U_x - U_y$, $\Delta^2 U_{xyab} = \Delta U_{xy} - \Delta U_{ab}$. In general, nth order differences are denoted by $\Delta^n U_i$, where i is an ordered set containing 2^n elements, which belong to X. Hence, $\Delta^n U_i = \Delta^{n-1} U_j - \Delta^{n-1} U_k$, where i contains the elements of j and k in that order.

Ordinality and cardinality are familiar concepts. If an individual's utility is ordinal then L consists of positive monotonic transformations only. In the case of cardinality, L consists of positive affine transformations only.

Ordinality   An individual's utility is ordinal if L is such that for all $\phi, U \in L$ and for all $x, y \in X, \phi_x > \phi_y \to U_x > U_y$.

Cardinality   An individual's utility is cardinal if L is such that for all $\phi, U \in L$, $U = a + b\phi$; for some a and $b, b > 0$.

It is important to note that the above definitions of ordinal and cardinal utilities are slightly weaker than those used in the current literature in welfare economics (Sen, 1970; Arrow, 1951; Fine, 1975). In this, ordinality requires that *only and all* positive monotonic transformations be permitted, whereas we require that *only* positive monotonic transformations be permitted. This weaker definition seems to be all that is required in many areas where the concept of ordinality has been used (e.g. indifference curve analysis) and is probably closer to what earlier authors intended it to be.

The distinction between these definitions is easily clarified with an example. Consider $x, y, z \in X$. Given ordinality, the welfare levels of these social states are comparable. Assume that x, y and z are preferred in that order. As far as utility differences between x and y, and y and z (i.e. the changes in utility caused by moving from y to x, and z to y) are concerned, they *may or may not* be comparable. Given strong ordinality (i.e. ordinality as defined by Arrow and Sen), not only are x, y and z ordered, but the utility difference between x and y, and y and z are *not* comparable. This ignorance of utility differences is a *necessary* part of strong ordinality, and hence the qualifying term 'strong'. It would perhaps have been more correct to refer to our definition as *weak* ordinality and the standard definition in welfare economics as simply ordinality. We refrain from doing so to keep the terminology simple. It will be obvious now that the stronger definition can be discarded for indifference curve analysis. An undesirable characteristic of strong ordinality is that if an individual's utility is cardinal then it is not strong ordinal. Similarly, our definition of cardinal utility, which Sen calls trans-cardinal, seems to be more useful and closer to the economic meaning of cardinality than the stronger definition.

Now, we study some of the properties of ordinal and cardinal utility with the aid of a numerical example. Assume $L = \{U, \phi\}, X = \{x, y, z\}$ and there are three individuals, 1, 2 and 3, represented by tables 1, 2 and 3.

	Table 1			*Table 2*			*Table 3*	
	U	ϕ		U	ϕ		U	ϕ
x	4	8	x	4	9	x	4	9
y	2	6	y	2	5	y	2	5
z	1	2	z	1	3	z	1	2

Ordinality implies that utility levels are comparable but first differences of utility (and higher-order differences) are not necessarily comparable. It is obvious that all three individuals have ordinal utility. However, individual 1 cannot compare first differences in utility. Consider the utility difference between x and y, and y and z for individual 1. Using U, we get $U_x - U_y = 2 > U_y - U_z = 1$. From ϕ, we get $\phi_x - \phi_y = 2 < \phi_y - \phi_z = 4$. Hence, individual 1 will not be able to say definitely whether the utility difference between x and y is larger than that between y and z or not. In the case of individual 2, $\phi = 2U + 1$. Hence, his utility is cardinal. It can be checked that his first differences of utility are comparable, the second-order differences (i.e. differences between differences) are comparable, and, in fact, nth order differences are comparable, for all values of n. This, as has been proved below, is a general property of cardinal utility. To summarise, given ordinality, first-order differences are not necessarily comparable but given cardinality nth order differences are comparable for all values of n.

The possibility of quasi-cardinal utility scales is immediately obvious. What about an individual who can compare all first-order differences but not necessarily higher-order ones, i.e. L consists of only those U and ϕ such that for all $i, j, r, s, \in X$, $\Delta\phi_{ij} > \Delta\phi_{rs}$ implies $\Delta U_{ij} > \Delta U_{rs}$. Similarly, a utility scale which requires second-order differences to be comparable is called quasi-cardinal of degree 2. Higher-order quasi-cardinalities may be defined along the same lines.

Quasi-cardinality of degree n (Q-card $n°$)[1]   An individual's utility is quasi-cardinal of degree n, if L is such that for all $\phi, U \in L$, and for all $k, j, \Delta^n \phi_k > \Delta^n \phi_j \rightarrow \Delta^n U_k > \Delta^n U_j$.

The utility of individual 3, represented by table 3 above, is Q-card $1°$. Certain other types of semi-cardinal scales have been proposed by Fishburn (1964) and others. But often the definitions have been cumbersome and unlike the quasi-cardinal scales above, have lacked intuitive appeal. The concept of 'the higher-ordered metric' measure, suggested by Seigel (1956) is logically equivalent to our Q-card $1°$.

Some interesting analytical results about the relationship between these different utility measures will now be stated.

Theorem 6*1   If an individual's utility is cardinal then it is ordinal.

That is, if L implies cardinal utility then it also implies ordinality. This is an obvious result and needs no proof.

Theorem 6*2   If an individual's utility is Q-card $1°$ then it is ordinal.

Theorem 6*3   If an individual's utility is Q-card $i°$, then it is Q-card $j°$, given $j < i$.

Theorem 6*4   If an individual's utility is cardinal, then it is Q-card $n°$, for every positive integer n.

These theorems make it clear that between the poles of ordinality and cardinality, there exists a whole sequence of quasi-cardinal scales such that each scale is stronger than all its predecessors. The converse of Theorem 6*4 is also true.

Theorem 6*5   If an individual's utility is Q-card $n°$ for every positive integer n, then it is cardinal.

This is a cardinalisation theorem, based on utility differences. Suppes and Winet's (1955) well-known theorem of cardinality is also based on utility differences. But their axioms were behaviouristic, and they did not assume the existence of numerically representable utility functions. Theorems 6*2–6*5 are proved in the appendix to this chapter.

The main relevance of utility measurement in the present context derives from its linkages with interpersonal comparability types and SWFs. Before delving into that a brief look is taken at some applications of quasi-cardinality.

Hicks (1939) argued that one of the main 'victims' of switching from Marshallian cardinal utility to ordinality was the concept of diminishing marginal utility (DMU). The principle of DMU demands the ability to compare first-order differences in utility, which ordinality lacks. There seems to be a dilemma in that DMU is an important concept in large areas of economics and its eschewal would mean a considerable loss to theory, and at the same time cardinality may seem too strong an assumption to make. A good compromise is Q-card $1°$ which provides just that

---

[1] This abbreviation is used both as an adjective and as a noun.

minimal strengthening to the ordinal scale which is necessary to reinstate the important principle of DMU.

Armstrong's (1939) analysis of 'indifference' has been discussed in Chapter 3. His theory requires that it be possible to speak of utility levels of alternatives as being 'close'. This led him to reject ordinality and invoke cardinality. It is now clear that Q-card $1°$ would have sufficed.

A fruitful application of quasi-cardinality is possible in the theory of risk. Here we discuss only some of the salient features of this, particularly how quasi-cardinality could lead to 'vagueness' in the preferences of a decision-maker. Given cardinal utility, preference is complete over all risky alternatives. If utility is ordinal, then preference is completely indeterminate. Quasi-cardinality, on the other hand, implies a quasi-determinate preference.

A simple example illustrates this. Let an individual face a choice between two risky alternatives, S_1 and S_2, where S_1 consists of a probability of $\frac{1}{2}$ each of getting social states x and z, and S_2 consists of state y for certain. Assume that $U_x < U_y < U_z$, for all $U \in L$. Which alternative is preferred by the individual? Assuming that individuals maximise expected utility, S_1 is preferred to S_2 if $\frac{1}{2}U_x + \frac{1}{2}U_z > U_y$, for all $U \in L$. If the individual's utility is strong ordinal, then clearly one can pick $\phi, \psi \in L$ such that $\frac{1}{2}\phi_x + \frac{1}{2}\phi_z > \phi_y$, and $\frac{1}{2}\psi_x + \frac{1}{2}\psi_z < \psi_y$. Hence his preference is incomplete over S_1 and S_2.

Does this necessitate that we go all the way to cardinality? Clearly not, for assume that the individual's utility is Q-card $1°$. Let $\frac{1}{2}\phi_x + \frac{1}{2}\phi_z > \phi_y$, for some $\phi \in L$. Hence, $\phi_x + \phi_z > 2\phi_y$, i.e. $\Delta\phi_{xy} > \Delta\phi_{yz}$. From the definition of the Q-card $1°$, it follows that $\Delta\psi_{xy} > \Delta\psi_{yz}$, (i.e. $\frac{1}{2}\psi_x + \frac{1}{2}\psi_z > \psi_y$) for all $\psi \in L$. Consequently his preference over S_1 and S_2 is complete.

If the alternatives were more complex than the above ones, Q-card $1°$ might have failed to generate a complete preference relation. Hence, quasi-cardinal utility implies an incomplete preference ordering. And this may be the main advantage of quasi-cardinality over cardinality. It allows for the fact that human beings may have some haziness in their preferences. This is also a sort of perception problem, albeit of a different kind from that discussed by Armstrong.

In the next section some comparability types are defined and their links with SWFs examined. Later we study the interconnections between concepts of measurement and comparisons.

Social welfare and interpersonal comparisons

Until recently, economists' opinion regarding interpersonal comparisons clustered around the two poles of complete comparability and no comparability at all (see Harsanyi, 1955 and Robbins, 1938, respectively). In recent years many different types of comparisons have been distinguished (Sen, 1970, 1977; Fine, 1974; Arrow, 1977) and here we define and study the properties of some of them. We begin with a sketch of certain social welfare functions which require different kinds of interpersonal comparisons.

Utilitarian ethics have been interpreted in various ways. Here we shall take it to imply a philosophy of maximising social welfare, where social welfare is a summation of individual utilities. Hence, as already pointed out in Chapter 2, the welfare from social state x is

$$W(x) = U^1(x) + U^2(x) + \ldots + U^n(x) \qquad (6.1)$$

and state y is preferred to x if and only if $W(y) > W(x)$ or $\sum_{i=1}^{n} [U^i(y) - U^i(x)] > 0$.[2] It is clear from this that utilitarianism requires some sort of ability to make interpersonal comparisons of *utility gaps* (e.g. $U^i(y) - U^i(x)$). Utilitarianism has its appealing aspects. It is a departure from 'deontological ethics' – a 'system which does not appeal to the consequences of our actions, but which appeals to conformity with certain rules of duty' (Smart & Williams, 1973, p. 5). Smart's defence of utilitarianism is basically along these lines. But there are many aspects of utilitarianism which makes it undesirable. The consequentialist framework, within which utilitarianism operates, may be severely restrictive, as argued by Williams (see Smart & Williams, 1973). What concerns us here is that this system of ethics can justify grossly inequitable distributions of income (Sen, 1973).

This shortcoming may be doctored by using a Bergson type SWF:

$$W = W(U^1, U^2, \ldots, U^n) \qquad (6.2)$$

with the requirement that it is strictly concave or that it satisfies some equity axiom, e.g. Sen's (1973) Weak Equity Axiom or Hammond's (1976, 1977) Equity Axiom. Informally speaking, equity axioms make judgements of the following nature. If an individual i is worse off than j in both states x and y, and i prefers x to y, then society should choose x over y (assuming that all members, other than i and j, are indifferent between x and y). It is immediately obvious that the application of equity axioms entail comparisons of *welfare levels*. Similarly the Rawlsian Maximum rule for social choice also requires level comparability (see Chapter 2).

So all these approaches require interpersonal comparisons, although of different types. In fact when it comes to governmental decision, there is usually no escape from interpersonal comparisons. The absence of explicit assumptions about comparability often means that there are

[2] In case there are many utility n-tuples which are permissible utility representations, then this inequality should hold no matter which representation is used. This will become more obvious later.

implicit ones. The relationship between SWFs and comparability concepts will be clear once we have taken a formal look at the notion of inter-personal comparisons.

Let X be the set of alternative social states. We assume that there are n individuals. Let each L^i, $i = 1, \ldots, n$, be the set of all real-valued functions that may be defined on X. Let $\mathbf{J} \subset \prod_{i=1}^{n} L^i$. Each element J^j of $\mathbf{J}$ is called a *functional combination* (Sen, 1970a) and represents a permissible combina-tion of utility functions of the n individuals. The extent of comparability is expressed by suitably defining $\mathbf{J}$. For an illustration of a particular $\mathbf{J}$ see the example on page 73. In this, J^1 and J^2 are the only permitted functional combinations. This means that in applying an SWF if individual 1 is represented by utility function ϕ^1, then individuals 2 and 3 must be represented by ϕ^2 and ϕ^3. If on the other hand individual 1 is represented by U^1 then the other two must be represented by U^2 and U^3. No other functional combination is permitted.

A definition of $\mathbf{J}$ implies some assumptions about the measurability of the individuals' utilities. How do we discover this implicit measurability of individual i's utility? $\mathbf{J}$ is a collection of ordered sets J^j. Consider the ith elements of all the sets contained in $\mathbf{J}$. Denote this set by $\bar{L}^i$. Technically, $\bar{L}^i$ is a *projection* of $\mathbf{J}$ onto the ith co-ordinate. At this stage there are two options. We could assume that (1) $\bar{L}^i$ contains exactly all the utility func-tions of individual i, or (2) $\bar{L}^i$ is a subset of the set containing exactly all the utility functions of individual i. The appropriateness of (1) or (2) depends on how broad we consider our framework of analysis to be. If we think of $\mathbf{J}$ as defining the framework of our analysis then (1) seems reasonable. If, on the other hand, we think of $\mathbf{J}$ as a definition in a broader framework, then $\bar{L}^i$ may be stricter than what is permitted by the measurability assumption as such, and in that case (2) would be more appropriate.

In what follows, we assume (1). Hence, every definition of $\mathbf{J}$ implies an $\bar{L}^i$, which is the set of exactly all utility functions of individual i. By using the definitions in the previous section, we can check what type of measurability is implied by $\bar{L}^i$. For example, let $\bar{L}^i$ imply Q-card $2°$. Then given (1), we would conclude that the ith individual's utility is Q-card $2°$. If, instead, we had assumed (2), then the individual's utility scale could be weaker than Q-card $2°$ (e.g. Q-card $1°$) since $\bar{L}^i$ would then be only a subset of his utility functions.

The same notations are used for utility functions, as in the last section, e.g. ϕ_x^A or U_x^A though now a superscript has been added to denote the individual it represents.

Consider two persons, A and B, among the n people. We want to know how their utilities compare. It is quite possible that, for one particular definition of $\mathbf{J}$, different pairs of people have utilities which are comparable up to different extents and in different ways. It should be clear that we are not assuming a 2-person society, but we are considering any two persons in an n-person society. Some concepts of comparability are defined formally and some theorems are established below.

Level comparability   Let $\phi^A, \phi^B \in J^i$; $U^A, U^B \in J^j$; $A \neq B$. If for all J^i, $J^j \in \mathbf{J}$ it is true that for all $x, y \in X$, $\phi^A > \phi^B \rightarrow U_x^A > U_y^B$, then A's and B's utilities are level comparable (LC).

Difference comparability   Let $\phi^A, \phi^B \in J^i$; $U^A, U^B \in J^j$; $A \neq B$. If for all $J^i, J^j \in \mathbf{J}$ it is true that for all $r, s, q, t \in X$, $\Delta \phi_{rs}^A > \Delta \phi_{qt}^B \rightarrow U_{rs}^A > U_{qt}^B$, then A's and B's utilities are difference comparable (DC).

Strong unit comparability   Let $\phi^A, \phi^B \in J^i$; $U^A, U^B \in J^j$; $A \neq B$. If for all $J^i, J^j \in \mathbf{J}$ it is true that for some a_A, a_B and $b, b > 0$, $U^A = a_A + b\phi^A$ and $U^B = a_B + b\phi^B$, then A's and B's utilities are strong unit comparable (SUC).

The concepts of LC and SUC have received considerable attention in the literature.[3] Informally, what DC means is that when A's and B's social states change, the two utility changes can be ordered, though the total utility levels of A and B or higher order differences may not be comparable.

Theorem 6*6   For any two individuals, SUC $\rightarrow$ DC.

The proof follows easily from the definitions.

In most applied welfare economics – e.g. cost–benefit analysis and also in our standard model, a simple additive SWF is assumed. The widespread use of a utilitarian framework is usually made without explicitly stating the assumptions of comparability and measurability. Now, we take a look at the assumption structure of utilitarianism.

$xR^a y$ means that utility of social state x, aggregated over individuals is at least as much as the aggregate utility of social state y for all permissible functional combinations. Formally,

$$xR^a y \leftrightarrow \sum_{i=1}^{n} [U_x^i - U_y^i] \geq 0, \text{ for all } [U^1, U^2, \dots, U^n] \in \mathbf{J}.$$

To say that utilitarianism is possible means that R^a is a complete ordering (i.e. it is a transitive, reflexive and complete relation). The next two theorems have been proved by Sen (1970) and hence they will not be proved here.

Theorem 6*7   For any $\mathbf{J}$, R^a is a quasi-ordering.

Though Sen proved this assuming 'ordinal-type' utility, such an assumption is not necessary. In fact individual utilities need not even be ordinal for R^a to be a quasi-ordering.

Theorem 6*8   If the utilities of all pairs of individuals are SUC, then R^a is a complete ordering.

---

[3] The definitions of LC and SUC in the economics literature (Sen, 1970; Fine, 1975) are slightly stronger than ours. If $\mathbf{J}^*$ implies SUC, as defined by Sen (1970), then we define utilities to be SUC if $\mathbf{J} \subset \mathbf{J}^*$. Similarly for LC.

Hence, given SUC, utilitarianism is possible. It will be proved below that SUC implies cardinal utility. From this there is a tendency to conclude that for utilitarianism cardinality is necessary. Such a conclusion is erroneous,[4] because SUC is a sufficient condition for utilitarianism and not a necessary condition (Sen, 1970). In fact not only is cardinality not necessary for utilitarianism but even ordinality is not necessary.[5] This is demonstrated with an example below.

An example

$X = \{x, y\}, n = 3, \mathbf{J} = \{J^1, J^2\}$. The chart below shows J^1 & J^2.

	J^1			J^2		
	ϕ^1	ϕ^2	ϕ^3	U^1	U^2	U^3
x	10	10	4	4	10	4
y	5	5	6	6	4	7

Considering J^1: $\displaystyle\sum_{i=1}^{3} [\phi_x^i - \phi_y^i] = 5 + 5 - 2 = 8 \geq 0$

Considering J^2: $\displaystyle\sum_{i=1}^{3} [U_x^i - U_y^i] = -2 + 6 - 3 = 1 \geq 0.$

Utilitarianism is possible, since $xR^a y$, i.e. R^a is a complete ordering, but ordinality is violated for individual 1 and SUC is violated for the pair of individuals 1 and 2. Consequently utilitarianism is possible without SUC and ordinality.

In a two-person society, DC is sufficient for utilitarianism.

*Theorem 6*9* In a two-person society, given DC, R^a is a complete ordering.

A corresponding theorem, however, does not hold in a society where $n \neq 2$. In the general case, while SUC is sufficient for utilitarianism, DC is neither sufficient nor necessary.

That ethically an equity conscious rule may be superior to utilitarianism has been extensively discussed by Sen (1973). Are there any practical reasons for supporting one rather than the other? Considering that to use an equity conscious rule it is necessary that utilities are LC, Sen (1973, p. 45) writes, 'In defending utilitarianism, therefore, one's best bet would be in making the rather peculiar assumption that utility differences

---

[4] Fine (1974) has shown how, given full-comparability and anonymity, as the extent of measurability is gradually strengthened the aggregation quasi-ordering becomes more and more complete and utilitarianism may be possible even before cardinality is reached. It ought to be noted that Fine's definition of full-comparability is different from Sen's (1970).
[5] In a one-person society, however, utilitarianism is possible, if and only if the individual's utility is ordinal.

are comparable [SUC] but levels are not.' It will now be argued that, provided an assumption is permitted, such a defence of utilitarianism is not possible. Given this assumption DC implies LC. Remembering that SUC implies DC, this means that whenever utilities are SUC, they must also be LC. This weakens the case for utilitarianism on practical grounds.

Assumption 1 There exists $s, r \in X$ such that for all $J^j \in \mathbf{J}$, $U_s^A = U_r^B$, where $U^A, U^B \in J^j$.

This assumption implies that there exists at least one level comparable pair. This coupled with DC implies that level comparability prevails over all social states.

Theorem 6*10 For individuals A and B, given assumption 1, DC $\rightarrow$ LC.

The relation between comparability and measurability

Different types of comparability often imply certain assumptions about measurability of individual utility. At times the relation is direct, and at other times only if certain assumptions are granted. With a set of theorems we establish some of these linkages.

Theorem 6*11 If A's and B's utilities are SUC, then A and B have cardinal utility scales.

At first sight it seems that DC implies Q-card $1°$. If you can compare your utility differences with another person's, you must be able to compare your own utility differences. However, there is no logical reason for this. A case where DC is satisfied but not Q-card $1°$ is demonstrated with an example.

An example

$X = \{x, y, z\}, n = 2, \mathbf{J} = \{J^1, J^2\}$. The chart below shows J^1 and J^2.

	J^1		J^2	
	ϕ^A	ϕ^B	U^A	U^B
x	8	0	8	0
y	6	0	7	0
z	5	0	5	0

$$\left. \begin{array}{l} 2 = \Delta\phi_{xy}^A > \Delta\phi_{yz}^A = 1 \\ 1 = \Delta U_{xy}^A < \Delta U_{yz}^A = 2 \end{array} \right\} \rightarrow \text{violation of } Q\text{-card } 1° \text{ for } A.$$

It is easily checked that DC holds.

Given an assumption, DC does imply Q-card $1°$.

Assumption 2

(a) for all pairs of first differences of A's utility, ΔU_{ij}^A and ΔU_{rs}^A, such that $\Delta U_{ij}^A \neq \Delta U_{rs}^A$, there exist $q, t \in X$ such that $\min\{\Delta U_{ij}^A, \Delta U_{rs}^A\} < \Delta U_{qt}^B < \max\{\Delta U_{ij}^A, \Delta U_{rs}^A\}$.

(b) Symmetric condition with A and B interchanged.

Theorem 6*12 Given assumption 2, if A's and B's utilities are DC then A and B have Q-card $1°$ utility scales.

The above theorem states that if the utilities of some individuals are DC and if assumption 1 is granted, then their utilities must be Q-card $1°$. This does not preclude the possibility that, even when assumption 1 is not fulfilled, the utilities are Q-card $1°$. And since it is unlikely that an individual's ability to compare his utility differences stems from the fulfilment or non-fulfilment of assumption 1, it may be reasonable, in practice, to assume utilities to be Q-card $1°$, whenever they are DC.

Though DC does not logically imply Q-card $1°$, it does imply ordinality.

Theorem 6*13 If A's and B's utilities are DC, then A and B have ordinal utility scales.

Intuitively it seems that LC utility should imply ordinality. If you can compare your own utility level with another person's, you should be able to compare your own utility levels in different social states. A counter-example shows that there is no logical reason for this.

An example

$X = \{x, y\}, n = 2, \mathbf{J} = \{J^1, J^2\}$. The chart below shows J^1 and J^2.

	J^1		J^2	
	ϕ^A	ϕ^B	U^A	U^B
x	10	2	20	2
y	20	2	10	2

$\left.\begin{array}{l} 10 = \phi_x^A < \phi_y^A = 20 \\ 20 = U_x^A > U_y^A = 10 \end{array}\right\} \rightarrow$ violation of ordinality.

It is easily checked that LC holds.

Assumption 3

(a) for all pairs of A's utilities, U_i^A and U_j^A such that $U_i^A \neq U_j^A$, there exists $q \in X$ such that $\min\{U_i^A, U_j^A\} < U_q^B < \max\{U_i^A, U_j^A\}$.

(b) Symmetric condition with A and B interchanged.

Theorem 6*14 Given assumption 3, if A's and B's utilities are LC, then A and B have ordinal utility scales.

The proof of this is similar to that of Theorem 6*12.

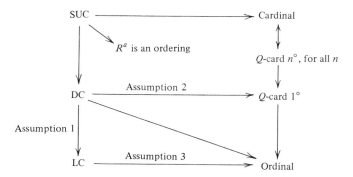

The implication diagram above links up the various concepts discussed. $A \xrightarrow{x} Y$ means $A \to Y$, provided x is satisfied.

It has been noted that the utilitarian framework is widely used in many areas of practical economics. This is also true for the standard model in Chapter 2, which uses a simple additive SWF. Unfortunately the informational requirements of utilitarianism have often been misunderstood. Some economists have, in recent years, tried to clear up these misunderstandings and in the above pages we have tried to do the same more rigorously. This has yielded some interesting results. Hence, it may be useful to conclude this section by recapitulating the results with the use of a simple Venn diagram. Let **J**-space mean a space within which each point represents a particular definition of **J**. If a particular **J**

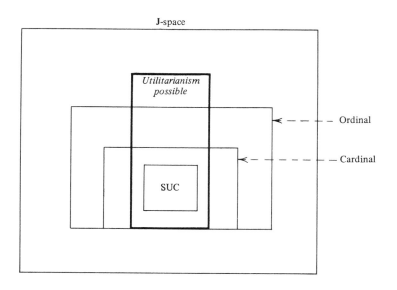

lies outside the area marked 'utilitarianism possible', then the preferences of a utilitarian decision-maker will not be completely determinate.

Quasi-cardinality and government preference

The question of measurability arises in two cases: (1) individual utility and (2) government's judgement of social welfare, which is usually considered to be a function of, among other things, individual utilities. In terms of equation (6.1) the measurability question arises for both U_is and W, though till now we have been discussing it mainly for the former.

Let us first consider (1). If a government's informational base is such that it has to treat the utilities of its citizens as quasi-cardinal rather than fully cardinal, then, as is obvious from Theorem 6*11 (and also the implication diagram), the government cannot make strong unit comparisons of interpersonal utilities. Since many SWFs are based on SUC this will mean indeterminateness in government preference. Though the lack of SUC does not necessarily wreck a utilitarian decision rule, it is likely to introduce incompleteness in government preference.

Now we come to (2). Let social welfare as judged by the government be Q-card t°, for some positive integer t. Under certainty this creates no problems. The government's indifference loci could still be a set of parallel hyperplanes in the O-space, since, for this, ordinality is sufficient. But what about risky situations, which are so pervasive in governmental decision-making? As argued earlier, for some risky alternatives the government will have well defined and consistent preferences. But for complex gambles the government's preference may be incomplete. Hence, in these areas the government's behaviour may be seemingly inconsistent. Of course, this can happen even if the government continues to be a maximiser of expected welfare. In a sense this is also a problem of perception. Unlike the case considered by Armstrong (1939), the government here may perceive welfare from riskless alternatives with perfect precision, but its perception may still lose its sharpness when it comes to complex risky alternatives.

Partial comparability and government preference

What will a government's neutral zones look like if it can only 'partially' compare interpersonal utilities? This is illustrated here in the case of a two-person society. But first we explain the meaning of partial interpersonal comparisons as defined by Sen (1970, 1970a). This is an important concept which frees us from the traditional shackles of extreme assumptions – full comparisons or no comparisons.

Partial comparability can be easily defined within the above framework.

We assume a two-person society. Consider any two utility functions (ϕ^1, ϕ^2) and call it the reference element, J^r, i.e. $J^r = (\phi^1, \phi^2)$. Let B be a convex cone, excluding the origin, in the positive orthant of E^2. Such a set may be referred to as a B-cone. Now a set of functional combinations can be defined as follows:[6] $(U^1, U^2) \in \mathbf{J}(J^r, B) \leftrightarrow$ there exists $[b_1, b_2] = \bar{b} \in B$, and some $[a_1, a_2]$ such that $U^1 = a_1 + b_1 \phi^1$ and $U^2 = a_2 + b_2 \phi^2$. It is clear that different types of $\mathbf{J}$ can be defined by suitably choosing J^r and B.

It can be easily proved that if B is a ray (excluding the origin) then utilities are SUC and, consequently, by Theorem 6*11, cardinal. If B is the entire positive orthant then $\mathbf{J}(J^r, B)$ implies completely non-comparable utilities. If B lies in between the entire positive orthant and a ray, then $\mathbf{J}(J^r, B)$ implies that the utilities of individual's 1 and 2 are *partially comparable*. This definition is generalisable to an n-person society (Sen, 1970a). The intuition of this definition is obvious. If B is a ray then for any particular positive number b_1 there is a unique number b_2 such that $[b_1, b_2] \in B$. Hence, if we multiply individual 1's utility function by b_1, we are permitted to multiply individual 2's utility function only by b_2. However, if B is the entire positive orthant then we can hold individual 1's utility function constant and blow up to any measure individual 2's utility. Clearly this implies non-comparability. If B lies between these two extremes as in Figure 6.1, then for any b_1 there is a range of permissible b_2s. So, for instance, if we multiply individual 1's

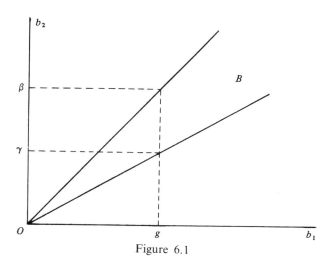

Figure 6.1

[6] It is worth noting that the reference element J^r is not necessarily an element of $\mathbf{J}(J^r, B)$. Only if $(1, 1) \in B$, then $J^r \in \mathbf{J}(J^r, B)$.

utility function (the reference one) by g, individual 2's utility function can be multiplied by any number between β and γ.

Now, given any $\mathbf{J}(J^r, B)$ we can define a strict preference relation P^a as follows:

$$xP^a y \leftrightarrow \sum_{i=1}^{2} [U_x^i - U_y^i] > 0, \text{ for all } (U^1, U^2) \in \mathbf{J}(J^r, B)$$

This is a utilitarian preference relation.[7] It implies that social state x is superior to y if and only if the aggregate utility in x is greater than the aggregate utility in y for all permissible utility functions. It follows from the definition of $\mathbf{J}(J^r, B)$, where $J^r = (\phi^1, \phi^2)$, and the above definition of P^a, that

$$xP^a y \leftrightarrow \sum_{i=1}^{2} b_i [\phi_x^i - \phi_y^i] > 0, \text{ for all } \bar{b} \in B$$

Let the relation of neutrality be denoted, as in Chapter 3, by N. xNy implies that the deciding agent has no reason to prefer one to the other as far as x and y are concerned.

$$xNy \leftrightarrow \text{not } xP^a y \text{ and not } yP^a x$$

$$\leftrightarrow \sum_{i=1}^{2} b_i [\phi_y^i - \phi_x^i] \geq 0, \text{ for some } \bar{b} \in B$$

$$\text{and } \sum_{i=1}^{2} b_i [\phi_y^i - \phi_x^i] \leq 0, \text{ for some } \bar{b} \in B$$

Now we want to see what the set $N(x)$ (i.e. the set of elements which are neutral to x) looks like in a 2-person economy, when utilities are partially comparable.

Let our reference utility functions be (ϕ^1, ϕ^2) and let B be a closed convex cone as in Figure 6.2. Let the set of all hyperplanes which have their normals in B be denoted by $T(B)$. In Figure 6.3 the two axes represented ϕ^1 and ϕ^2. The social state x is represented by (ϕ_x^1, ϕ_x^2) in Figure 6.3. The neutral zone, $N(x)$, given partial comparability defined by B in Figure 6.3, is $T(B)$ with the vertex transferred to x, i.e. $N(x) = x + T(B)$. It is easy to see why this should be so. Consider any z such that $z = (\phi_z^1, \phi_z^2) \in x + T(B)$ as shown in Figure 6.3. Hence $z - x \in T(B)$. Therefore, there exists $\bar{b} \in B$ such that $z - x$ is orthogonal to $\bar{b}$, i.e. $b_1 [\phi_z^1 - \phi_x^1] + b_2 [\phi_z^2 - \phi_x^2] = 0$. From the definition of N, it follows that zNx.

Hence, given partial comparability, we can no longer assume linear neutral zones as in the standard model. Neutral zones (in two dimensions)

---

[7] If P^a is a strict preference relation then $xP^a y$ implies x is preferred to y. Note that P^a is not the asymmetric part of R^a as defined above.

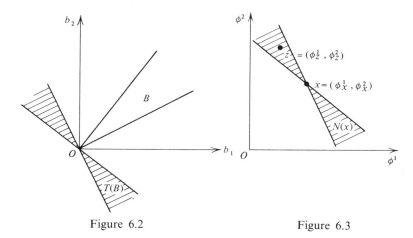

Figure 6.2   Figure 6.3

are cone complements. Assume that the government considers, using the terminology of the standard model, B^1 and B^2 to represent the welfares of two groups, but feels that there can be other representations of welfares as well, such that B^1 and B^2 act as reference elements and allow a class of functional combinations in the manner described above. Then neutral zones are cone complements and only the *generalised* model can be used to evaluate the government's preference.

In the case of *n*-person societies, while any B-cone which is not just a ray implies a 'haziness' in preference, some restrictions need to be imposed on Sen's (1970a) general B-cones for them to imply neutral zones which are representable by cone complements. But we shall not go into this here. It is interesting to observe some of the connections between B-cones and neutral zones in the 2-dimensional case. Let there be two cones $\bar{B}$ and $\bar{\bar{B}}$ and let $\bar{N}(x)$ and $\bar{\bar{N}}(x)$ be the corresponding neutral zones. If $\bar{B} \subset \bar{\bar{B}}$, then $\bar{N}(x) \subset \bar{\bar{N}}(x)$ and if $\bar{B}$ is a ray, then $\bar{N}(x)$ is a hyperplane. Hence, as the government's ability to compare interpersonal utilities becomes sharper, the degree of precision (see Chapter 3) increases, the extreme being reached when the neutral zone is a hyperplane as in the standard model.

It ought to be mentioned that while we have derived the above results assuming an unweighted additive SWF, similar results may be obtained even if benefits of different groups or individuals are weighted differently as in our earlier models.

Appendix to Chapter 6

*Theorem 6*2* If an individual's utility is Q-card $1°$ then it is ordinal.

    Proof Consider any $\phi \in L$. Let $\phi_s > \phi_r$, for some $s, r \in X$. Hence,

$\phi_s - \phi_s > \phi_r - \phi_s$. This implies that for all $U \in L$, $U_s - U_s > U_r - U_s$, since L defines a Q-card $1°$ utility scale. Hence, for all $U \in L, U_s > U_r$. Therefore the utility scale is ordinal.

Theorem 6*3 If an individual's utility is Q-card $i°$ then it is Q-card $j°$, given $j \le i$.

Proof All we need to prove is that Q-card $(n + 1)° \rightarrow Q$-card $n°$. Hence, starting from any $\phi \in L$, we have to prove that if for all i, j and for all $U \in L$,

$$[\Delta^{n+1} \phi_i > \Delta^{n+1} \phi_j] \rightarrow [\Delta^{n+1} U_i > \Delta^{n+1} U_j]$$

then for all k, l and for all $U \in L$,

$$[\Delta^n \phi_k > \Delta^n \phi_l] \rightarrow [\Delta^n U_k > \Delta^n U_l]$$

Noting that $\Delta^{n+1} \phi_t = \Delta^n \phi_r - \Delta^n \phi_s$, for some s and r, it is clear that the proof of this is no different from the proof of Theorem 6*2.

Theorem 6*4 If an individual's utility is cardinal, then it is Q-card $n°$, for every positive integer n.

Proof Cardinality implies that for any $\phi \in L, U = a + b\phi$, for some a & $b, b > 0$, for all $U \in L$. Hence, $\Delta U_{xy} = b\Delta\phi_{xy}, x, y \in X$. It follows, by induction on n, that $\Delta^n U_i = b\Delta^n \phi_i$, for all n. This implies that $\Delta^n \phi_i > \Delta^n \phi_j \rightarrow \Delta^n U_i > \Delta^n U_j$, for all i, j, for all n and for all $U \in L$.

Theorem 6*5 If an individual's utility is Q-card $n°$, for every positive integer n, then it is cardinal.[8]

The proof of the theorem is easier to follow once we have established the following lemma.

Lemma 1 Let $f : B \rightarrow R$, where R is the set of real numbers and $B \subset R$. It is given that for $s_i, t_i \in B, i = 1, 2, \ldots, r$,

$$\sum_{i=1}^{r} f(s_i) > \sum_{i=1}^{r} f(t_i) \leftrightarrow \sum_{i=1}^{r} s_i > \sum_{i=1}^{r} t_i, \text{ for all } r \qquad (1)$$

If $S_1, S_2, T \in B$, and $\alpha + \beta = 1$, then

$$T = \alpha S_1 + \beta S_2 \rightarrow f(T) = \alpha f(S_1) + \beta f(S_2)$$

Proof α and β are either both rational numbers or neither is, since $\alpha + \beta = 1$.

(i) Assume both are rational. Then α and β can be written as $\frac{p}{r}$ and $\frac{q}{r}$ respectively, where p, q and r are integers ($r \ne 0$). Hence $T = \alpha S_1 + \beta S_2$

$\rightarrow \quad rT = pS_1 + qS_2$

---

[8] This proof is shorter than and different from my original one and was suggested to me by Professor Binmore.

→ $rf(T) = pf(S_1) + qf(S_2)$, by (1), noting that $q + p = r$, since $\alpha + \beta = 1$

→ $f(T) = \alpha f(S_1) + \beta f(S_2)$

(ii) Assume α and β are not rational. Then consider sequences $\{\alpha_n'\}, \{\alpha_n''\}$, $\{\beta_n'\}, \{\beta_n''\}$ of rational numbers such that

(a) the former two converge to α, and the latter two to β

(b) $\alpha_n'' + \beta_n'' = 1$, for all n; and $\alpha_n' + \beta_n' = 1$, for all n; and

(c) $\alpha_n' S_1 + \beta_n' S_2 < \alpha S_1 + \beta S_2 = T < \alpha_n'' S_1 + \beta_n'' S_2$

It follows in the same way as in (i), that

$$\alpha_n' f(S_1) + \beta_n' f(S_2) < f(T) < \alpha_n'' f(S_1) + \beta_n'' f(S_2)$$

Now
$$\lim_{n \to \infty} \alpha_n' f(S_1) + \beta_n' f(S_2) = \lim_{n \to \infty} \alpha_n'' f(S_1) + \beta_n'' f(S_2)$$
$$= \alpha f(S_1) + \beta f(S_2)$$

Therefore, $f(T) = \alpha f(S_1) + \beta f(S_2)$

Now, we are prepared to tackle the theorem directly.

Proof Let an individual's utility be Q-card $n°$, for all n. Hence, if $\phi, U \in L$, then

$$\Delta^n \phi_k > \Delta^n \phi_l \leftrightarrow \Delta^n U_k > \Delta^n U_l, \text{ for all } n \qquad (2)$$

(2) can be expressed more simply as

$$\sum_{i=1}^{r} \phi_{x_i} > \sum_{j=1}^{r} \phi_{y_j} \leftrightarrow \sum_{i=1}^{r} U_{x_i} > \sum_{j=1}^{r} U_{y_j}, \text{ for all } n \qquad (3)$$
$$\text{where } r = 2^n$$

the social states having been renamed $x_1, \ldots, x_r$ and $y_1, \ldots, y_r$. Since the utility scale is ordinal, the indifference classes for ϕ and U are the same. Pick one element from each indifference class and obtain a set Y. Then $\phi: Y \to R$ and $U: Y \to R$ are 1:1 functions. Let $B = \phi(Y)$ and consider $f: B \to R$ defined by $f(s) = U(\phi^{-1}(s))$, where $s \in B$.

It follows from (3) that

$$\sum_{i=1}^{r} s_i > \sum_{i=1}^{r} t_i \leftrightarrow \sum_{i=1}^{r} f(s_i) > \sum_{i=1}^{r} f(t_i), \text{ for all } n$$
$$\text{where } r = 2^n$$

Suppose $S_1, S_2, T \in B$ such that $T = \alpha S_1 + \beta S_2$, and $\alpha + \beta = 1$. It follows from Lemma 1, that $f(T) = \alpha f(S_1) + \beta f(S_2)$. Hence, f is an affine function on B. Therefore, $f(s) = bs + a$, for all $s \in B$.

i.e. $u(\phi^{-1}(s)) = bs + a$

Let $x = \phi^{-1}(s)$. Then $U(x) = b\phi(x) + a$

Now, $b > 0$, for otherwise ordinality would be violated.

Theorem 6*9 In a two-person society, given DC, R^a is a complete ordering.

Proof In view of Theorem 6*7, we merely have to prove the completeness of R^a. Consider any $\phi^A, \phi^B \in J^i \in \mathbf{J}$. Assume, $\Delta\phi_{rs}^A + \Delta\phi_{rs}^B \geq 0$, for some $r, s \in X$.

$\rightarrow$ $\Delta\phi_{rs}^A \geq \Delta\phi_{sr}^B$

$\rightarrow$ $\Delta U_{rs}^A \geq \Delta U_{sr}^B$, for all $J^j \in \mathbf{J}$, where $U^A, U^B \in J^j$, since DC is assumed

$\rightarrow$ $\Delta U_{rs}^A - \Delta U_{rs}^B \geq 0$

$\rightarrow$ $rR^a s$

Now, clearly for any J^i, either $\Delta\phi_{rs}^A + \Delta\phi_{rs}^B \geq 0$ or $\Delta\phi_{sr}^A + \Delta\phi_{sr}^B \geq 0$. Hence either $rR^a s$ or $sR^a r$.

Theorem 6*10 For individuals A and B, given assumption 1, DC $\rightarrow$ LC.

Proof For some $\phi^A, \phi^B \in J^i \in \mathbf{J}$, let $\phi_i^A > \phi_j^B$. By assumption 1, there exist $s, r \in X$, such that $\phi_s^A = \phi_r^B$. Hence, $\Delta\phi_{is}^A > \Delta\phi_{jr}^B$. This implies that $\Delta U_{is}^A > \Delta U_{jr}^B$, for all $J^i \in \mathbf{J}$, where $U^A, U^B \in J^i$, since DC is assumed to hold. Hence, $U_i^A > U_j^B$, for all $J^i \in \mathbf{J}$, since by assumption 1, $U_s^A = U_r^B$.

Theorem 6*11 If A's and B's utilities are SUC, then A and B have cardinal utility scales.

Proof Let A's and B's utilities be SUC. Consider A. Let J^i be any element of $\mathbf{J}$. Let $\phi^A \in J^i$. Given SUC, for any $J^i \in \mathbf{J}$, if $U^A \in J^j$, then $U^A = a_A + b\phi^A$, for some a_A & $b, b > 0$. Hence, each element of $\bar{L}^A$ is a positive affine transformation of all elements. Hence A's utility is cardinal. Similarly for B.

Theorem 6*12 Given assumption 2, if A's and B's utilities are DC then A and B have Q-card $1°$ utility scales.

Proof We shall only consider A. Symmetric arguments apply to B. Let $\phi^A, \phi^B \in J^i$, where J^i is any element of $\mathbf{J}$. Let $\Delta\phi_{ij}^A > \Delta\phi_{rs}^A$. By assumption 2, there exist $q, t \in X$ such that

$$\Delta\phi_{ij}^A > \Delta\phi_{qt}^B > \Delta\phi_{rs}^A$$
$\rightarrow$ $\Delta U_{ij}^A > \Delta U_{qt}^B > \Delta U_{rs}^A$, for all $J^j \in \mathbf{J}$, because of DC

$\rightarrow$ $\Delta U_{ij}^A > \Delta U_{rs}^A$, for all $J^j \in \mathbf{J}$

Theorem 6*13 If A's and B's utilities are DC, then A and B have ordinal utility scales.

Proof For any $J^i \in \mathbf{J}$ and $\phi^A, \phi^B \in J^i$, let $\phi_x^A > \phi_y^A$. Hence, $\Delta\phi_{xy}^A > 0$. Now, for any $r \in X$, $\Delta\phi_{rr}^B = 0$. Therefore, $\Delta\phi_{xy}^A > \Delta\phi_{rr}^B$, which implies $\Delta U_{xy}^A > \Delta U_{rr}^B$, for all $J^j \in \mathbf{J}$, since DC is assumed. But $\Delta U_{rr}^B = 0$. Hence $\Delta U_{xy}^A > 0$, which implies $U_x^A > U_y^A$, for all $J^j \in \mathbf{J}$. A similar proof holds for B.

7

Interdependence and revealed preference

Interdependence among agents can drive a wedge between an agent's preference and its revelation. And in such circumstances, to elicit preference from observed behaviour may require insights into the workings of an agent's mind, which would be very difficult to acquire in reality. We shall use the Prisoner's Dilemma (PD), a two-person non-zero-sum game, to highlight the problems of interdependence. The reasons for choosing this particular game are many. This game has been discussed widely in economics, philosophy and psychology.[1] It has important applications in everyday life and helps us to understand some of the difficulties in rational decision-making in general. The PD could also underlie some situations of political conflict as will be demonstrated in the next chapter. The inherent logic of this game is also of interest and there remain some unresolved problems to one of which we turn briefly later.

The Prisoner's Dilemma

The Prisoner's Dilemma is usually posed as an anecdote. A police chief offers two prisoners the following options. If they both confess to the crime they are being accused of, they will be imprisoned for ten years each. If neither confesses, then they will get two years each. If however, one confesses and the other does not, then the one to confess gets zero years in jail and the other gets twenty years. To keep the story simple, we assume that the prisoners are held in separate rooms (though this assumption is not essential) and asked to confess or not confess. What should each prisoner do? It is immediately obvious that each individual can do better for himself by confessing, no matter what the other does. Hence, rational individuals will confess and get ten years each in jail. But if each had not confessed, then they would have got two years each. Clearly, individual rationality is in conflict with group rationality. This is the dilemma.

[1] For example, in Luce and Raiffa (1957) and articles by Sen and Watkins in Korner (1974). It has been claimed that the antecedents of the PD game go back to Rousseau and Hume. In Mill (1848, pp. 329–32) one gets a lucid discussion of the PD type of interaction.

Now, to pose the same problem shorn of these anecdotal details, consider two agents A and B, who have open to them two strategies each, a_1 and a_2, and b_1 and b_2 respectively. The pay-off matrix is as shown below. α_{ij} (resp. β_{ij}) is the pay-off to A (resp. B) for (a_i, b_j).

B

	b_1	b_2
a_1	α_{11}, β_{11}	α_{12}, β_{12}
a_2	α_{21}, β_{21}	α_{22}, β_{22}

A (label to the left of the rows)

For simplicity, assume the pay-offs to be monetary payments. Hence, if A plays a_1 and B plays b_2 then A gets £α_{12} and B gets £β_{12}. It will be assumed throughout that individuals maximise monetary gains.

Consider the following assumptions:

$$\alpha_{21} > \alpha_{11} > \alpha_{22} > \alpha_{12} \tag{i}$$

$$\beta_{12} > \beta_{11} > \beta_{22} > \beta_{21} \tag{ii}$$

Individual A (resp. B) is said to have PD preference if (i) (resp. ii) holds. We assume throughout that both A and B have PD preferences. It is easy to see that if this game is played once, then (a_2, b_2) is the equilibrium outcome. This is Pareto inferior to (a_1, b_1). Therefore, if this sort of a preference configuration occurs in reality, as seems quite plausible, then a Pareto indifferent outcome seems inevitable.

Intra-governmental interdependence

The PD sheds light on the sort of error liable to occur if the government is treated as a single agent – as is usual not only in revealed preference analysis, but in most of economic theory.

Let a government consist of two ministers, A and B, whose strategies interact as in the PD above. The chosen alternative will then be (a_2, b_2). Now, by ignoring the process by which the government arrives at (a_2, b_2), if we treat the government as a single agent who chooses (a_2, b_2) rather than – among other alternatives – (a_1, b_1) and infer that the government prefers (a_2, b_2) to (a_1, b_1), we shall clearly be wrong. This point is so obvious that it would not have been worth mentioning, were it not for the fact that there are many works on government behaviour which totally ignore the group character of government.

That intra-governmental conflicts of this nature are not theoretical games but a distinct possibility in reality is obvious once we consider an example: Two ministers are responsible for undertaking one part each of a potential two-part project. Given the general public's ignorance about the details of the internal mechanisms of government, it is very likely that whether the project is undertaken in full, in part or not at all, both ministers are held equally responsible and receive equal bouquets or brickbats. In such a situation it is quite possible that (1) A and B prefer that the project is undertaken in full rather than not at all, and (2) whether B (resp. A) undertakes his part or not, A (resp. B) prefers not to undertake his. The possibility of this occurrence can be illustrated numerically. Assume that if the project is undertaken in full, in either part or not at all, each minister gets laurels from the citizens worth 10, 5 or 0 utils, respectively. To undertake a part of the project requires that 7 utils of effort be expended. If it is not undertaken, then 0 utils of effort are spent. These are realistic figures; and it may be checked that, given these, (1) and (2) are satisfied. This creates a PD situation and the project is not undertaken. From this to infer that the government prefers not to undertake the project will be incorrect.

Governments and other agents: the iterated game

A different problem arises when the conflict is between the government and some other agent like a big business organisation or another nation.

In the above game let the government be A and the other agent B. If the government selects strategy a_i, then the revealed preference analyst will infer that, according to A's preference, either (a_i, b_1) is at least as good as (a_j, b_1) or (a_i, b_2) is at least as good as (a_j, b_2) or both. If the game is played once then the government will select a_2 and the inference of the analyst will be correct.

However, in reality many games are played more than once. Suppose that the agents know that the above game will be played more than once. Then A might play a_1 a few times to induce B to play b_1. Once B gets the hint and plays b_1, the equilibrium might settle at (a_1, b_1). A (resp. B) would not break this equilibrium, since, though by suddenly playing a_2 (resp. b_2) he can reap some extra gains, B (resp. A) will retaliate with b_2 (resp. a_2) making A (resp. B) eventually worse off.[2] In this case it therefore becomes a distinct possibility that even though assumption (i) holds, A will play a_1.

From this, the revealed preference analyst may be led to conclude that either α_{11} is at least as large as α_{21} or α_{12} is at least as large as α_{22} or both. And indeed he will be wrong. It is clear that this problem is not created by interdependence alone. It is interdependence coupled with the fact that an agent might behave sub-optimally today to induce the other agent to behave in such a way in future that he may reap greater benefit in the long run.

---

[2] For a more detailed exposition of this see Luce and Raiffa (1957), p. 98. There have been many studies of the iterated Prisoner's Dilemma in recent years, e.g. Rapoport (1967), Schick (1977).

Now, it has been argued by Luce and Raiffa (1957, pp. 98–9) that in the case where the PD is repeated a finite number of times, and the players know how many times, the equilibrium will continue to be (a_2, b_2), i.e. A will not move a_1 in any game.

It will be shown that this argument is not, in general, valid.[3] A will certainly move a_2 only if a set of assumptions about A's knowledge of B, A's knowledge of B's knowledge of A, and so on are granted. This dependence of A's behaviour *not only* on his preference (i.e. (i) on p. 85) *but also* on his knowledge of B and higher order knowledges, makes it virtually impossible to unravel his preference from his behaviour.

Let us first consider the Luce and Raiffa argument as to why (a_2, b_2) must be the equilibrium strategy in the case of finitely iterated PD.

Suppose the players are told that game H [i.e. the above game] is to be played exactly twice, and suppose that each player is shrewd enough to see that his second strategy strictly dominates his first one in a single play of the game. Thus, before making their first move, each realizes that in the second game the result is bound to be (a_2, b_2), for, after the first game is played, the second one must be treated as if H is going to be played once and only once. The second play being perfectly determined, the first play of the game can be construed as H being played once and only once. Thus, it appears that (a_2, b_2) must arise on both trials. The argument generalizes: Suppose they know that H is to be played exactly 100 times. Things are clear on the last trial, the (a_2, b_2) response is assured; hence the penultimate trial, the 99th, is now in strategic reality the last, so it evokes (a_2, b_2); hence the 98th is in strategic reality the last, so it evokes (a_2, b_2) etc. This argument leads to (a_2, b_2) on all hundred trials. Indeed if player 2 is a b_2-conformist on all trials, then player 1 is best off choosing a_2 on all trials, and conversely, i.e., (a_2, b_2) on all trials is an equilibrium pair [Luce and Raiffa, pp. 98 and 99].

From the above argument it seems that given the assumption that the two individuals have PD preferences, the equilibrium is (a_2, b_2) whether the game is played once or any finite number of times. It will be argued that this is incorrect. The mere assumption that A and B have PD preferences is sufficient to establish (a_2, b_2) as the equilibrium in the single game case. But when the game is repeated $N(>1)$ times, the assumption requirement is much stronger. This can be seen by carefully analysing the case of N games.

Consider the case of $N = 2$. Luce and Raiffa argued that in the first game A will move a_2 because A knows that in the final game (a_2, b_2) is bound to occur. But how does A know that? Clearly, to know that, A must know that B has PD preference. Symmetrically, B must know that A has PD preference. Therefore, to prove (a_2, b_2) to be the equilibrium in the first game we need this additional assumption that A (resp. B) knows that B (resp. A) has PD preference.

[3] The ensuing analysis has been published in Basu (1977). For further elaboration see Schick (1977).

Now, even if $N = 100$, this assumption is necessary since, without it, we would not be able to prove that (a_2, b_2) would certainly occur in the 99th game. Hence, for all $N > 1$, this assumption is necessary. But is this assumption sufficient for all N? The answer is no. As N becomes larger, the list of assumptions increases.

Consider $N = 3$. We can be sure that A will move a_2 in the first game if he thinks that outcomes of games 2 and 3 are fixed. A will think in this way if (1) A knows that B has PD preference (this will make A sure that the final game's outcome will be (a_2, b_2)) and (2) A knows that B knows that A has PD preference. This will make A sure that B will move b_2 in the second game, and consequently makes him sure that the outcome of the second game will be (a_2, b_2). Remember that because of (1), A will move a_2 in the second game. Given that symmetric conditions hold for B, the outcome of the first game will be (a_2, b_2).

The increasing informational assumption is obvious. We now summarise the above analysis.

When $N = 1$, (a_2, b_2) is the equilibrium if
  A and B have PD preferences.
When $N = 2$, (a_2, b_2) would certainly occur in both games if
  A and B have PD preferences, and
  A (resp. B) knows that B (resp. A) has PD preference.
When $N = 3$, (a_2, b_2) would certainly occur in all three games if
  A and B have PD preferences, and
  A (resp. B) knows that B (resp. A) has PD preference, and
  A (resp. B) knows that B (resp. A) knows that A (resp. B) has PD preference.

What happens in the general case where $N = n$? The result is summarised in the chart overleaf. It is assumed in it that both A and B have PD preferences.

The chart clarifies that while in the case of non-repeated PD the suboptimal solution is a direct consequence of the individuals having PD preferences, in the n-game case it is not so.

While people are often confronted with PD situations in life, it is not at all clear that they can be expected to fulfil assumptions (1), (2)...$(n-1)$ and $(1^*), (2^*)...((n-1)^*)$. These are extremely strong informational requirements. When these assumptions are not satisfied, the occurrence of (a_1, b_1) in some games becomes a distinct possibility.

When these assumptions are granted we can be sure that an agent will not choose an alternative which is sub-optimal to him in the immediate game just in order to influence the other agent's ensuing moves, because the outcomes of all future games are determined anyway. But in case any of these assumptions is not fulfilled, then an agent's behaviour becomes a resultant of preference over outcomes and certain subjective probabilities.

	A moves a_2 if the following additional assumptions are given:	B moves b_2 if the following additional assumptions are given:
nth time	No additional assumptions.	No additional assumptions.
$(n-1)$th time	(1) A knows B has PD preference.	(1*) B knows A has PD preference.
$(n-2)$th time	(1) and (2) A knows that (1*).	(1*) and (2*) B knows that (1).
$(n-3)$th time	(1), (2) and (3) A knows that (1*) and (2*).	(1*), (2*) and (3*) B knows that (1) and (2).
$(n-(n-1))$th time (i.e. 1st time)	(1), (2) ... $((n-2))$ and $((n-1))$ A knows that (1*), (2*) ... and $((n-2)^*)$.	(1*), (2*) ... $((n-2)^*)$ and $((n-1)^*)$ B knows that (1), (2) ... and $((n-2))$.

So to elicit preference from behaviour, information regarding subjective probabilities will be necessary.

It is worth noting that the assumption structure we have just explored is of wider interest. Decision-theorists dealing with interdependence in finitely iterated PD have had a slight feeling of unease because of the Luce and Raiffa result which rules out any interdependence. They normally bypassed this problem by assuming that while in principle the Luce and Raiffa result held, it did not hold in practice. From the above analysis it is now clear that even in principle the Luce and Raiffa argument does not hold unless the above assumptions are granted.

What is an individual's optimal strategy if the assumptions are not granted? There has been some recent work in this area (Rapoport, 1967; Schick, 1977). There are essentially two classes of iterated games: the finitely iterated and the infinite ones. We demonstrate the nature of interaction involved by considering a twice repeated game.

The Prisoner's Dilemma with interpersonal uncertainty

We assume $N = 2$; A and B have PD preferences and in situations of uncertainty they maximise their individual *expected* earnings; $\alpha_{ij} = \beta_{ji}$, for all i, j (i.e. A and B have symmetric pay-offs); and A's expectation of B's behaviour is the same as B's expectation of A's behaviour. These last two assumptions are not really necessary but are made to allow us restrict our analysis to one individual, since the other will behave symmetrically. Finally, no assumptions like $(1),(2)\ldots((n-1))$ and (1^*), $(2^*)\ldots((n-1)^*)$ are granted.

Since A and B have PD preferences, (a_2,b_2) is bound to occur in the final game. Hence, our main interest lies in the first game. Consider the subjective probabilities attached by A to B's moves. The probability of B moving b_2 in the first game is r. If in game 1 A moves a_2, then the probability of B playing b_2 in the second game is p. If in game 1 A moves a_1, then the probability of B playing b_2 in the second game is q. If A moves a_2 in game 1, it is natural for him to expect retaliation from B in the second game. So we assume $p > q$.

Let A's expected gain from playing a_1 in the first game be $G(1)$. Hence,

$$G(1) = (1-r)\alpha_{11} + r\alpha_{12} + (1-q)\alpha_{21} + q\alpha_{22}$$

Similarly, the expected gain from playing a_2 in the first game is $G(2)$.

$$G(2) = (1-r)\alpha_{21} + r\alpha_{22} + (1-p)\alpha_{21} + p\alpha_{22}$$

In both these expressions, the first two terms are expected earnings from game 1, and the last two terms are expected earnings from game 2. Because of our assumption above, B's subjective probabilities regarding A's behaviour are symmetric. Hence, a similar analysis applies to B.

Let $X = G(1) - (G(2)$. Therefore,

$$X = (1-r)(\alpha_{11} - \alpha_{21}) + r(\alpha_{12} - \alpha_{22}) + (p-q)(\alpha_{21} - \alpha_{22})$$

If $X > 0$, then A plays a_1 in game 1; and if $X < 0$, then A plays a_2. If $X = 0$, then A's move is indeterminate in the context of this theory. It is easily checked that suitable values for the parameters can be selected such that (i) (see page 85) is satisfied and at the same time $X > 0$. Hence it is possible for A to have PD preference and at the same time move a_1 in the first game. B's behaviour being symmetric, the occurrence of (a_1,b_1) is a distinct possibility. Thus behaviour in the first game may not directly reflect preference. Assumption 1 (p. 89) says that $p = q = 1$. If this holds, then $X < 0$ and, in keeping with the analysis in the previous section, A will move a_2 in both games.

In the light of our analysis in Chapter 6 it may be interesting to note that if the pay-offs were in utilities and A's utility scale happened to be ordinal then X could be greater than, equal to or less than zero for different elements of L^A – the set of all permissible utility functions. This would mean that while in the last game the individual would have a definite preference between a_1 and a_2, his preference would be indeterminate in the first game. Cardinality, or perhaps even quasi-cardinality of some degree, would prevent such indeterminateness.

Before moving on to the next topic a few remarks on infinitely iterated games would not be out of order. A major problem with the infinite PD is that we can no longer simply 'sum up the utilities of the conditional consequences of the options, stage over stage. There may be an infinite number of meetings, and so all the sums may be infinite' (Schick, 1977). There are many ways out of this (e.g. see Shubik, 1970) and a particularly simple one, that adopted by Heal (1976), is to assume that the players meet once a year to play the PD and that they have a positive discount rate. This goes on for an infinite number of years. He first considers a strategy S_A according to which A will move a_1 only as long as B moves b_1. If B also adopts a similar strategy then A's total pay-off will be (r is the discount rate)

$$\sum_{t=1}^{\infty} \frac{\alpha_{11}}{(1+r)^t} = \text{(say) } Y$$

What happens if A suddenly breaks the (a_1, b_1) equilibrium and moves a_2? Then B will retaliate by playing only b_2. And A's sequence of pay-offs will be as follows

$$\alpha_{11} \dots \alpha_{11} \, \alpha_{21} \, \alpha_{22} \dots \alpha_{22} \dots$$

So A will suddenly move a_2 only if the present value of this sequence is greater than Y.

This is a very simple analysis and has many shortcomings. For example, it is extremely unrealistic to assume permanent retaliation from the players, as done in Heal's analysis. However, the model serves the purpose of giving one a flavour of the kind of interaction involved in infinitely iterated games.

In the next chapter political constraints are studied. It will be shown how the root of political constraints may lie in a PD type of relationship between the citizens of an economy.

8
Feasibility constraints

When a government is observed to choose a project from a given set, it is important to know which subset of it consisted of the feasible projects. If x was chosen and y rejected, then a meaningful rejection inequality (see Chapter 2) may be formed only if y was feasible. If y was infeasible, then no information regarding government preference is transmitted by its choice of x.

A feasible set consists of exactly those elements which satisfy all constraints – both technical and political. In the previous chapters, feasible sets were referred to without specifying what the relevant constraints were. If it is always known which projects have been rejected *on grounds of infeasibility*, then an understanding of the nature of the constraints may be dispensable in evaluating governmental weights. However, in reality, while technical constraints are usually easy to handle, ambiguity surrounds the notion of political feasibility. This could happen because of both theoretical and practical reasons. The theoretical problem stems from the fact that political infeasibility could have degrees. This means that there could exist projects which cannot be classed as totally infeasible. The practical problem arises because governments often prefer to keep in obscurity the actual reasons for rejecting a project. These factors combine to make the task of identifying the politically feasible projects a formidable one. Also, till now it was assumed that the choice of projects depends on their ultimate characteristics (i.e. their endowments in terms of the government's objectives). The *process* of generating a particular objective vector was deemed irrelevant. In politics, however, this is very important. The same objective vector could be both feasible and infeasible depending on the process used to arrive at it.

Before going into the main issues of political feasibility, a common theoretical fallacy needs to be cleared.

Constraints and cost–benefit analysis: a theoretical problem

Eckstein (1958) argued that it was only common sense that in cost–benefit analysis the 'with and without principle' (WWP) should be employed. This principle requires us to consider two worlds over the planning period – one assuming project p_i is undertaken and the other without project p_i. The welfare generated by the former world, minus that by the latter, is the welfare of project i. This method, however, leads to a problem. The following statement is common in planning: 'Welfare from project p_1 is greater than 0, but p_1 cannot be implemented as it is infeasible.'

If the WWP was used to evaluate the welfare of p_1, then the above statement is contradictory. p_1 is infeasible means that a world with p_1 is not possible. This makes it impossible to evaluate the welfare of p_1 by the WWP. Hence, it is not possible to say that 'welfare from project p_1 is greater than 0'. Eckstein (1958) argued that all projects should be evaluated by the WWP, but later considered the possibility that some projects with net welfare greater than 0 may have to be rejected because of budget constraints. This is clearly open to the above criticism.

There are also practical reasons for not using the WWP. In order to focus our attention on only certain aspects of projects, it may be sensible to evaluate the welfares of the projects, pretending that certain constraints do not exist. For example, if we are only interested in the economic aspects of a project, we may pretend that no political constraints exist. Then we consider two worlds, not like the actual ones, but ones where political constraints do not exist – one with the project and one without – and then subtract the welfare of the latter world from the welfare of the former to get the welfare of the project. Then obviously a project may have net welfare greater than zero and still be rejected on grounds of infeasibility because it may be violating the political constraint.

Eckstein had to consider the budget constraint after project welfares had been evaluated because he calculated the welfares of projects pretending the absence of budget constraints. This principle of evaluating net welfares by considering two worlds, but with the additional requirement that some constraints, which exist in reality, are assumed absent in these worlds, will be called the modified with and without principle (MWWP). What Eckstein was in fact using was the MWWP.

In the previous chapters when we spoke of the 'welfare of a project', we did not do so in the sense of the WWP or the MWWP. The prevailing benefit vector of the economy was subtracted from the benefit vector of the economy with the project (pretending some constraints do not exist); and then the SWF was applied to find the project's welfare. The criterion for project choice, in this case, is also different from that associated with the MWWP. p_1 is chosen not if $W(p_1) > 0$ as would be the case if $W(p_1)$ was evaluated by the MWWP, but if $W(p_1) \geq W(p_i)$ for all feasible p_i. No matter whether this method of evaluation or the MWWP is adopted, the same projects will be chosen as long as the underlying SWF is the same one.

Political constraints

A political constraint is often thought of as a partition of the k-dimensional O-space[1] into two subsets – the politically feasible and infeasible. The process by which the particular point in the O-space is generated is considered irrelevant in this context. But even if we ignore the process there are enough difficulties. It will be argued that political constraints are often woven into the government's preference so that it is no longer clear what its 'pure' preferences are. When a government decides on a particular location for a project a part of its choice may well have been guided by political considerations like the party's prospects in the next election. In such cases it might not be possible to differentiate between 'pure' preference and political factors. Moreover, there is also the more basic question of the meaningfulness of 'pure' preferences. It should be mentioned at the outset that by the very nature of the topic it is difficult to use rigorous techniques and make conclusive propositions; and we do not attempt to do either.

We begin by examining the implications of the simplistic view that a political constraint merely partitions E^k into the feasible and infeasible. Let Π denote the set of politically feasible $\bar{B}$ vectors. Hence, $\Pi \subset E^k$. A planning problem can typically be expressed as follows.

Formulation 1 $\max W = \sum_{i=1}^{k} a_i B_i = \bar{a}\bar{B}$

subject to (1) $\bar{B} \in \Pi$
            (2) the non-political constraints

This means that planning is an attempt to maximise some SWF subject to some constraints – both political and technical, i.e. (1) and (2) respectively. If this was all there was to it, then the problem would simply be that of identifying Π. We shall, however, argue that political constraints are more complex in that they affect the nature of the SWF. But before delving into that we need to examine more closely the meaning of political feasibility.

Two plausible definitions are as follows: (A) If the generation of $\bar{B}$ by the ruling party implies that the electorate will overthrow the ruling party, then $\bar{B}$ is termed politically infeasible. Let X be the set of all such $\bar{B}$s. (B) If the generation of $\bar{B}$ is an impossibility because of the people's opposition (e.g., if all workers in an area refuse to participate in the construction of a steel plant and also do not allow workers from outside to do so) then $\bar{B}$ is politically infeasible. Let Y be the set of all such $\bar{B}$s.

If (A) is accepted, then Π is the complement of X in E^k. Given (B), Π is the complement of Y. Though X and Y are related in that both have to do

---

[1] For the meaning of O-space see Chapter 2.

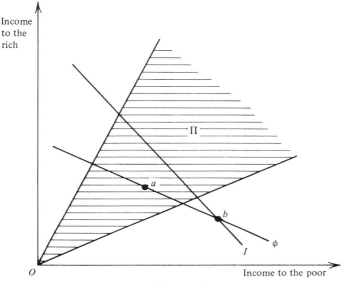

Figure 8.1

with people's dissension, they will be distinct sets. There could exist a governmental action, e.g. a sterilisation program, which the ruling party can carry out, but if it does so, it loses the following election. In most of the traditional economics literature *both* (A) and (B) seem to be accepted, i.e. a project is described as politically infeasible if it lies in either X or Y. However, the appropriateness of describing the elements of X as infeasible is open to question, since the projects in X *can* be undertaken and if they are not it is only because the government *prefers* not to lose elections. Though most of the ensuing discussion does not hinge on any specific definition of Π, it will be convenient to assume (B).

In Figure 8.1 let the shaded area represent Π and let I be the actual indifference curve of the government. All other indifference curves are parallel to I.

Clearly, if the government faces a choice between implementing either a or b, then it will choose a. If the economist is ignorant of political infeasibility, then he will infer from this that the slope of the indifference curves is less steep than ϕ. This would be an error. The Weisbrod model faces this danger.

The UNIDO approach may bypass this problem. In this procedure the minister, being subjected to verbal choice only, may ignore political constraints. He may genuinely not know what will meet with public opposition. Moreover, there is something ignoble about not doing the 'right' thing and succumbing to pressures and a minister may not admit that he would not do the right thing if he knew that his answer was merely a verbal one (not leading to actual implementation). If this is true, then if the minister is asked to choose between a and b, he will choose b, and the economist would infer correctly that the indifference curve is steeper than ϕ. However, this is clearly not a surefire method of bypassing the problem. And moreover, a technique which is not based on actual behaviour will have many other shortcomings.

Consequently, the only way is probably to try and somehow directly determine the politically feasible region and then to apply revealed preference techniques. This, of course, will have serious practical difficulties. But even if one is prepared to waive these, one confronts formidable theoretical problems. This arises from the fact that in the real world the line dividing the feasible and infeasible zones will not be a line at all but a hazy band.

To inject this dose of realism into our analysis we need to rewrite formulation 1 in the following manner:

Formulation 2   max $W^0 = F(\bar{B})$

subject to the non-political constraints. F is defined such that if $\bar{B} \in \Pi^c$, where Π^c is the complement of Π in E^k, then $F(\bar{B}) = -\infty$ and if $\bar{B} \in \Pi$, then $F(\bar{B}) = \sum_{i=1}^{k} a_i B_i$, as in formulation 1.

The meaning of this is easy to explain in words. It is an alternative way of looking at formulation 1. It merely suggests that instead of looking at Π^c as an infeasible region, we can think of it as a region of infinite disutility.[2]

Till now, it has been assumed that (*a*) the government knows Π^c and (*b*) political dissent makes it impossible to tread into Π^c, which could be alternatively expressed by saying that it gives infinite disutility to the government to tread into Π^c.

In a more realistic model (*a*) and (*b*) are untenable. Few governments know with certainty what projects will meet with public dissent. As one of the relatively more discerning characters of P. G. Wodehouse comments – 'In all human schemes – and it is this that so often brings failure to the subtlest strategists – there is always the chance of the Unknown Factor popping up, that unforeseen X for which we have made no allowance and which throws our whole plan of compaign out of gear.'[3]

Governments, while ignorant of the exact nature of Π, are usually aware of the Wodehouse dictum. So it could be reasonably assumed that a government has a hazy idea of Π and its disutility increases as Π^c is

[2] Forms 1 and 2 are equivalent in the sense that if we had to choose one project from a set S, then both formulations would lead to the same choice, provided the following assumption is granted: There must exist at least one project in S such that the $\bar{B}$ associated with it satisfies constraints 1 and 2 of formulation 1.
[3] *The Heart of a Goof*, P. G. Wodehouse, Penguin, 1926, p. 144.

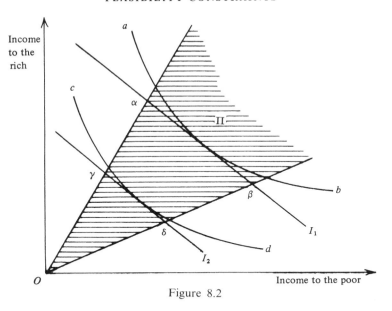

Figure 8.2

approached, just as a blind man slows down as he approaches a familar wall.

Moreover, that there are two regions – one where there is no dissent and one may enter, and another which is *impossible* to tread into because of political dissent (i.e. Π^c) – is also unrealistic. Instead of thinking of a well defined set like Π^c it is more realistic to think of a zone where the deeper one treads, the greater the political dissent and, consequently, the greater the disutility to the government.

What all this means in terms of government preference is now clarified geometrically. Assume first that political constraints do not exist, i.e. $\Pi = E^2$, (i.e. the entire O-space, assuming there are only two objectives, as in Figure 8.2). Then the indifference curves are I_1 and I_2. Now let political constraints be created and let Π be the zone of no dissent. According to formulation 2, the indifference loci are $\alpha\beta, \gamma\delta$ and the unshaded region where welfare is negative infinity. But according to the above argument the indifference curves will look like *ab* and *cd*. Hence, in the absence of political considerations I_1, I_2 are the indifference curves but if the government takes political dissent into account the indifference curves are like *ab* and *cd*.

Let us denote the SWF associated with *ab* and *cd* by W^*. As before, the SWF associated with I_1 and I_2 is W. What we argued above is that given a set of projects, a government will have two orderings on it – one given by W and one by W^*. The antenna of revealed preference analysis may pick up W or W^* or a mixture of the two, causing obvious difficulties. When searching for the implicit government preference one should first be clear which ordering one is looking for and then look for a suitable revealed preference technique. If we analyse preferences purely from actual past choices we shall pick up W^*, since the associated indifference curves are the actual behaviour lines. On the other hand, $\alpha\beta$ and $\gamma\delta$ are hypothetical constructs of what would be the preference if political considerations were absent. It is possible that, politics being such a part and parcel of governmental decision-making, no technique can properly capture $\alpha\beta$ and $\gamma\delta$. And in that case the very meaningfulness of 'pure' preferences such as those represented by $\alpha\beta$ and $\gamma\delta$ may be questionable.

A further point worth stressing is that two governments which have identical indifference curves when political constraints are ignored, may have separate indifference curves when they take political considerations into account – even though they may be operating in identical political milieux. This is so because the two governments' beliefs and expectations about the political impacts of projects may differ. In other words, political parties make different choices, not always because their ideologies or preferences are different, but because they *perceive* the political realities differently.

It is now clear that a political constraint can no longer be thought of as a simple partition of all benefit vectors into feasible and infeasible ones. Political dissension affects the very nature of the government's SWF rather than merely constraining its area of application. This makes it much more difficult to separate out the effects of politics on economic decisions. While this model is more realistic than the initial simple one, it still has the shortcoming of not attaching any significance to the process of generation of particular benefit vectors. And this, as already mentioned, is important where political constraints are concerned. The next section is devoted to this question.

Taxes and political feasibility

Let $\bar{B}$ be the benefit vector generated by both projects p_1 and p_2. Whereas p_1 generates $\bar{B}$ directly, p_2 generates $\bar{B}$ through a basic project accompanied by some tax transfers. In terms of the government's SWF, p_1 is as good as p_2, because the process of creation of a benefit vector is irrelevant. That tax transfers often meet political resistance is a generally accepted fact. So it is possible that while p_1 is politically feasible, p_2 is not. Hence, the same point in the O-space may be politically feasible or infeasible depending on the process by which that point is arrived at. It is also possible that $\bar{B}^j > \bar{B}^i$ but project p_j is rejected because it involves certain politically unpalatable taxes. If the government actually tries to implement $\bar{B}^j$, faces dissent, and then rejects it, then there is no problem for the revealed preference analyst. But frequently a government decides in advance which projects are infeasible and rejects them straight away. This may give the wrong impression that the government prefers the chosen project to the rejected ones.

While most economists are aware of the fact that tax transfers may be thwarted politically, little effort has been expended on explaining the basis of such behaviour. The conditions under which the imposition of an income tax would be politically infeasible are worth discussing. It provides insight into the more general problem of political forces constraining economic decisions. It demonstrates how in a society of rational individuals, political forces could, under certain circumstances, impede even Pareto efficient changes.

We begin by considering a case where the imposition of an additional income tax, and the consequent increase in government expenditure, is 'beneficial' to society on the aggregate. Then we analyse the different lobbies which will tend to be formed in reaction to this potential tax. There will be different types of anti-tax lobbies stemming from different aspirations. We distinguish between these and examine the nature of interaction between them.

Let S be the set of all citizens. We assume that S has s elements. We shall be conducting our analysis at the margin. Consequently S (and, by extension, s) is fixed. Members of this society pay some taxes, consume public goods and private goods, etc. Now, the government plans a new tax of t per person from each individual in a set $N \subset S$. Let N consist of n individuals. Hence, the total new tax is equal to nt. Assume that the government spends the entire new tax on providing public goods.[4] Now, a public good is such that each man's consumption is the entire amount of the good, i.e., in this case, nt amount of goods. How much utility a person gets from a public good is determined according to his tastes (Samuelson, 1955). Let b_i be the utility to individual i from one unit of public good. Hence, the total satisfaction is $\sum_{i \in S} b_i nt$. Let d_i be the disutility to individual i from one unit of tax. Hence, the total disutility from this new tax is $\sum_{i \in N} d_i t$. Assuming a utilitarian government, the SWF is a linear one and the total utility generated by this tax, and the consequent government expenditure, is $\sum_{i \in S} b_i nt - \sum_{i \in N} d_i t$, or $\sum_{i \in S \setminus N} b_i nt + t \sum_{i \in N} (b_i n - d_i)$.[5]

Since the analysis will be carried out at the margin, it seems reasonable to assume (i) d_i and b_i are constants, for all i. We also make the reasonable assumption that (ii) $d_i, b_i > 0$, for all i. Since we are interested in examining

---

[4] Both the assumptions of uniform taxation and expenditure on exclusively public goods could be relaxed without upsetting our conclusions.

[5] The set $X \setminus Y$ consists of exactly those elements of X which are not in Y.

how a socially desirable tax may be politically impeded, we begin by assuming that this new tax is socially beneficial, i.e.

$$\sum_{i \in S \setminus N} b_i nt + t \sum_{i \in N} (b_i n - d_i) > 0 \qquad (1)$$

Now, we take a look at different types of anti-tax behaviour. The most discussed category is of the tax-evaders (Srinivasan, 1973). If every individual in N pays this new tax but $i \in N$ evades it, then his net benefit will be $b_i(n-1)t$. Let X_i be the difference between the benefits he gets if he evades the tax and if he pays it.

$$X_i = b_i(n-1)t - (b_i nt - d_i t) = t(d_i - b_i) \qquad (2)$$

Hence,

$$E = \{i \in N \,|\, X_i > 0\}$$

consists of the set of potential *tax evaders*. Whether they actually evade taxes or not will depend on many factors, like the efficiency of the government's enforcement machinery. However, given that people maximise utility, members of E will prefer not to pay taxes. We shall assume, what would seem reasonable in most societies, that all tax payers would prefer to evade taxes, i.e. (iii) $E = N$.

The second type of anti-tax behaviour stems from being a net loser as a consequence of the tax. Clearly, (1) does not negate the possibility that for some $i \in N$, $b_i nt - d_i t < 0$. Hence, the set

$$L = \{i \in N \,|\, (b_i nt - d_i t) < 0\}$$

is termed the *losers' lobby*.

Let G (gainers) be the set of all individuals in N who do not lose as a result of this new tax. Hence,

$$G = \{i \in N \,|\, (b_i nt - d_i t) \geq 0\}$$

In terms of the theory of the 'core' (see Luce and Raiffa, 1957), if L is non-empty, then it is said that this new tax is 'blocked'. However, in reality, the mere non-emptiness of L does not imply that the new tax will be prevented from being imposed. Firstly, it is quite possible that the members of L, in spite of being losers, do not pick up the cudgels against the government's proposal of this new tax. Secondly, a government does not depend on the voluntary co-operation of everybody before making a move. Because of (1) the government thinks that the tax is beneficial, and moreover the persons in G and $S \setminus N$ (the non-tax-payers) support the tax. So it is a tussle, with the government, $S \setminus N$ and G on one side, and L on the other. Hence, as far as the imposition of this new tax goes the crucial question is not the existence or non-existence of losers, but the strength of their lobby.

In most writings there seems to be a preoccupation with the behaviours of the tax evaders and the losers' lobby. But these are intuitively obvious and require little analysis. Moreover, authors, e.g. Sei (1961), give the impression that the existence or non-existence of a ceiling on income tax depends on the strength of the losers' lobby. This is, however, incorrect. It is possible that even if L was an empty set (i.e. the new tax was a Pareto efficient one), the tax would be blocked. To see this we turn to the third and the most interesting type of anti-tax behaviour.

It will be demonstrated that though in a vote on whether to have the tax or not, G would vote in favour of it, the members of G will tend to form identifiable political groups and lobby for tax exemption of their respective groups, and may even be responsible for having the tax scheme rejected. Though we are here concentrating on G, similar groups or lobbies may be formed even among members of L. We assume that tax evasion is not possible.

Let M be a subset of G, and let it consist of r number of citizens. For simplicity we assume that people within M have the same preferences, i.e. $b_i = b$ and $d_i = d$, for all $i \in M$. If this group gets tax exemption, while all others continue to pay taxes, then for an individual $i \in M$, the net benefit is $b_i(n - r)t$. Let Z_i be the net benefit accruing to i if M gets tax-exemption, minus the net benefit to i if M does not get the exemption.

$$Z_i = b_i(n - r)t - (b_i nt - d_i t) = t(d_i - b_i r) \tag{3}$$

Let r^* be that value of r for which $Z_i = 0$. It is easy to prove the following: (a) $1 < r^* \leq n$, and (b) if r is such that $1 \leq r < r^*$, then the Z_i corresponding to the r is greater than 0.

(a) Given the constancy of t, d_i and b_i, it is obvious that Z_i is a linear function of r. If $r = 1$, then $Z_i = X_i$. But $X_i > 0$, for all i, by assumption (iii). Hence, if $r = 1$, then $Z_i > 0$. Since $i \in G$, therefore $b_i nt - d_i t \geq 0$, i.e. $t(d_i - b_i n) \leq 0$. Hence, if $r = n$, then $Z_i \leq 0$. Therefore, $1 < r^* \leq n$.

(b) This follows directly from the fact that Z_i is a linear function of r and that $X_i > 0$.

It follows from (b) that if M is a group of size between 1 and r^*, and if it succeeds in getting tax-exemption, then the members of the group will benefit. The smaller the value of r, the larger the gains of each member in the group. This follows from (3). On the other hand, the larger the group, the greater the possibility of a successful lobby for tax-exemption. Hence, the individuals will try to form themselves into groups of sizes somewhere between 1 and r^* and lobby for their respective groups' tax exemption. Such groups will be called the *exemption lobbies*.

The interaction between this group, M, the losers' lobby, L, and the government is an intricate one. Assume that M is successful in getting the tax exemption. Now, consider a member k of $G \backslash M$. Since k is an element of G, we know that initially when the new tax was proposed, he was a gainer, i.e. $b_k nt - d_k t \geq 0$. But after M gets tax exemption, the net benefit to k from the tax scheme will be $b_k(n - r)t - d_k t$. This is less than $b_k nt - d_k t$, and it is quite possible that $b_k(n - r)t - d_k t < 0$, in which case k moves from G to L. Hence, it is quite possible that M getting the tax exemption will result in some members of $G\backslash M$ moving to L, thereby strengthening L – the lobby in favour of tax removal altogether.

What is more important is that the government may decide not to impose the tax, even without any lobbying by L, merely in anticipation of M's behaviour. This is easy to see. If M gets exemption, then the social welfare from the tax scheme is $\sum_{i \in S} b_i(n - r)t - \sum_{i \in N\backslash M} d_i t$. It is possible that this expression is negative, though (1) holds. This means that the alternatives: (A) everybody pays the tax, (B) nobody pays the tax, and (C) everybody except M pays the tax, will be preferred in that order by the government. If, after considering the new tax scheme, the government feels that M is a powerful group and consequently (A) is an impossibility, then the government chooses the second best, which is (B), i.e. the government does not even raise the issue of a new tax. And the members of M, who prefer (C), (A) and (B) in that order, therefore, as a consequence of their own power, land up with their worst option. This outcome is a consequence of interdependence between the government and M working through the former's *anticipation* of the latter's behaviour. Clearly, this can happen without any pressure from L. In fact, L could be an empty set. Examples of this sort of interaction abound in everyday life. A mother who brings chocolates home and would like to give her son one piece but not two (since that would affect his health adversely) may be forced to refrain from giving any, out of fear that once her stubborn son has had one, there would be no way of stopping him from having another.

The above analysis raises an interesting question about power. It demonstrates how an agent can end up with a less preferred alternative by the very virtue of its power. Though this may seem inconsistent at first sight, this is a very realistic possibility. M is powerful, at least 'potentially' powerful[6] – since he has the *capability* of getting his own way, as far as the choice between (A) and (C) is concerned. And it is this very fact which (via the government's anticipation of his power) leads to his getting his worst alternative, namely (B). One question which arises is that if M is powerful enough to force the choice of (C) from the pair (A) and (C), why cannot it coerce the government to reject (B)? The answer lies in the fact that (B) is the status quo and coercing the government to move from (B) to (A) or (C) involves breaking the status quo and making others pay the new tax. Clearly this requires much greater power than is required to earn an exemption for oneself, i.e. move from (A) to (C). Hence, it is not surprising if an agent succeeds in forcing the government to choose (C)

---

[6] For an excellent discussion of this concept and power in general see Lukes (1974).

from between (A) and (C) but fails to make it reject (B). Of course, this is not to deny that there could be agents which are powerful enough to perform both.

Preferences and the Prisoner's Dilemma

Having discussed the Prisoner's Dilemma in the previous chapter, it may be interesting to study the structure of preferences of the members of G in game-theoretic terms. It will be seen that the interaction of preferences between the members of G is of the Prisoner's Dilemma type.

Let I stand for individual i and R for all others. Let the subscripts 0 and 1 stand for not-paying and paying taxes, respectively. Now, consider $i \in G$. From the definition of G it follows that i prefers $I_1 R_1$ to $I_0 R_0$. $I_1 R_1$ represents the case where i pays the tax and so do all others. $I_0 R_0$ may be interpreted similarly. Since, by assumption, $X_j > 0$, for all j, therefore i prefers $I_0 R_1$ to $I_1 R_1$. Now, $X_i > 0$ also implies $t(b_i - d_i) < 0$. Hence, if i pays his tax and no one else pays, i.e. $I_1 R_0$, then the net benefit to i, $tb_i - td_i$, is less than 0. If no one pays the tax, i.e. $I_0 R_0$, then the net benefit to i is 0. Hence, i prefers $I_0 R_0$ to $I_1 R_0$. The alternative can now be expressed in order of i's preference as follows:

$$I_0 R_1 \quad I_1 R_1 \quad I_0 R_0 \quad I_1 R_0$$

This is the Prisoner's Dilemma type of preference. All members of G have this type of preference. It should be noted that the Prisoner's Dilemma discussed here is an n-person analogue of what is actually a 2-person game.

A penalty for tax-evasion could alter the preference pattern. Moreover, in reality this game situation would be arising repeatedly, and the equilibrium in an iterated Prisoner's Dilemma may be the socially optimal one (see Chapter 7). This dynamic aspect has been ignored above, and may be worth pursuing. Also, under slightly different assumptions, the number of citizens, s, could be important in determining the preference of an individual. Then by manipulating s – which can be done by breaking up the economy into many sectors, which are isolated as far as tax collection and expenditure go – it may be possible to break out of the sub-optimal equilibrium. These matters require a much more detailed enquiry.

The aim of the above analysis was a limited one. It demonstrated how, in an economy consisting of rational individuals, political forces may be generated such that economically desirable alternatives turn out to be infeasible. It also illustrated the importance of the *process* of generating a particular benefit vector. We constructed an extremely simplified model to demonstrate these points. A more realistic model would have to take into account many other factors and would be much more complex.

9
Some practical issues

What are the practical uses of revealed weights? The present chapter looks into this and concludes with suggestions for further work and a summing up of the enquiry undertaken in this book.

Uses of revealed weights

The purpose of a critique is frequently not to wreck a model but to render it more useful by exposing its drawbacks and preventing wrong applications of it. It is clear from the preceding chapters that there are quite a few blemishes in the theoretically elegant models for evaluating government preference. This entails a considerable curtailment of the area of application of these techniques as compared to what was envisaged by earlier authors.

The main purpose of revealed preference analysis seems to have been to derive a set of weights which could be used in public sector decision-making. Pointing out the need for an SWF for cost–benefit analysis (CBA) and policy-making, Mera (1969) writes, 'Such a welfare function can be derived from decisions made by a public body if several assumptions are granted.' This possibility was suggested earlier by Eckstein (1961) and motivated most of the subsequent models for revealing government preference. The pages which span the space between the standard model and here raise doubts about the use of revealed weights for CBA.

It is true that for cost–benefit analysis some value parameters are required, and to reject revealed weights as candidates leaves us with the question: Whose values and what sort of weights do we use in public decision-making? This is a controversial question and we do not attempt to give any positive answer here. But it is worth pointing out that some of the alternatives to political weights which have been suggested are not very compelling. It is also important to note that to reject *revealed* weights does not imply a rejection of governmental value judgements, which can be used in CBA in ways other than through revealed weights.

In a rather philosophical criticism of the UNIDO approach, Mishan (1974) argues against the use of politically determined parameters for cost–benefit analysis. He correctly stresses the human shortcomings of bureaucrats and the fact that they seldom truly represent the nation. And he goes on to suggest that economists should restrict themselves to the traditional approach based on the *potential Pareto principle*. According to this approach, 'the cost–benefit criterion is met if the algebraic sum of the aggregate compensating variations is positive'. But what is so ethically appealing about this criterion? Mishan does not try to answer this question. Indeed, when it comes to the question of distribution, this approach does not even have the virtue of Paretian reticence, but passes judgements which may support gross inequalities.

Mishan is aware that there may be areas where the economist 'encounters difficulties in evaluating some particular social benefit or cost item'; and he suggests that in such cases the economist 'has the option of leaving its calculation out of the analysis', meaning that these gaps will be filled in by the political process.

But then he falls prey to his own argument – aimed at the UNIDO approach – that 'once politically determined valuations are believed pertinent to some agenda, there is no obvious case for limiting the extent of political intervention for this purpose ... There seem to be no logical reasons against going further, and having political decisions over-ride all market prices and individual valuations' (Mishan, 1974, p. 93).

These confusions merely reveal the deep-seated problems which remain in this area. As already mentioned, we shall not take any more than the negative stand that there is good reason for scepticism in using *revealed* governmental value-parameters. And, anyway, the use of revealed values does not fully cure the problems of cost–benefit analysis caused by the absence of value parameters. This is more formally explained below.

First let us see in what sense value parameters are necessary for CBA. Let X be a set of potential, independent projects. The purpose of CBA is to describe an ordering over X with the help of an implicit or explicit SWF. In line with the rest of the book let the welfare, $W(p_i)$, from project p_i be given by the following linear function:

$$W(p_i) = \bar{a}\,\bar{B}^i \qquad (9.1)$$

If we are given a set $\Omega^t \subset E^k$, within which $\bar{a}$ must lie, then corresponding to Ω^t we can define a preference relation R^t, as follows: For $p_i, p_j \in X$, $p_i R^t p_j \leftrightarrow [W(p_i) \geq W(p_j)$, for all $\bar{a} \in \Omega^t]$. This means that one project is declared as good as another if and only if it generates greater welfare (in the weak sense) no matter which $\bar{a}$ is chosen within a predefined set.

Now assume that no value parameters are known. This means that $\bar{a}$ can take any value, i.e. $\Omega^t = E^k$. In this case R^t will have no power to distinguish between projects. For all pairs $p_i, p_j \in X, i \neq j$, neither $p_i R^t p_j$ nor $p_j R^t p_i$. This is what is meant by saying that cost–benefit analysis is not possible if no value parameters are specified. There is a theoretically important exception to this rule. If p_i and p_j are such that in spite of being different projects their benefit vectors are identical, then $p_i R^t p_j$ *and* $p_j R^t p_i$. In what follows we ignore this possibility. Also, if we impose the *a priori* restriction of $\bar{a} > 0$, then a preference quasi-ordering is obtained over X, which is equivalent to the vector-dominance quasi-ordering.

What happens if precise value parameters are specified, i.e. Ω^t is a singleton?[1] It can be easily proved that in such a case R^t will be a complete ordering. This is what is meant by saying that given precise value parameters, CBA is possible. In this case, given finiteness of X, the existence of a choice set is guaranteed, and CBA makes it possible to locate this set.

The nature of revealed weights is such that their use in CBA will normally lead to a situation in between the two polar cases just considered. If Ω^t is a set of revealed weights then it will in general lie somewhere between E^k and a singleton set in E^k. In fact very often Ω^t will be a substantial subset of E^k. What does this imply about the nature of R^t? It is intuitively obvious and can be easily proved that if Ω^t is non-empty and $\Omega^t \subset E^k$, then R^t will be a quasi-ordering. Moreover, if $\Omega^s \subset \Omega^t$, then $p_i R^t p_j$ implies $p_i R^s p_j$. This implies that as the set of possible weights shrinks, the relation R^t becomes more complete. It ought to be noted that R^t will not be a sub-relation of R^s unless some additional assumptions are granted.

The main results so far discussed are summarised below:

If $\Omega^t = E^k$, then for no $p_i, p_j \in X, i \neq j, p_i R^t p_j$.

If Ω^t is a singleton, and $\Omega^t \subset E^k$, then for all $p_i, p_j \in X$, $p_i R^t p_j$ or $p_j R^t p_i$.

If $0 \neq \Omega^t \subset E^k$, then there may exist some $p_i, p_j \in X$, such that $p_i R^t p_j$, and there may exist some $p_i, p_j \in X$, such that neither $p_i R^t p_j$ nor $p_j R^t p_i$.

This makes it clear that if the success and failure of CBA are associated with R^t being complete or incomplete over every pair in X respectively, then (compared to the case where no weights are used) the use of weights evaluated by the type of revealed preference models discussed in this book moves us from failure towards success, but not necessarily up to it.

There are of course other approaches which allow us to derive exact weights (i.e. Ω^t is a singleton or a ray) but these models require an even heavier load of assumptions. Recently there has been an attempt to derive a set of exact weights for Kenya. This work of Scott, MacArthur and Newbery (1976) is of particular interest and relevance because the study was motivated by the need to use income weightings in CBA. It also brings to light the compromises one is forced to make in undertaking empirical analysis. The authors stress the importance of the distributional objective and write, 'A total which gives the same value to each £1 of benefit, no matter to whom it accrues, implicitly makes the assumption that they are of equal value, which can easily be shown to be

---

[1] It is not necessary for Ω^t to be a singleton. The same result holds if it is a single ray through the origin (see p. 15).

implausible if it is meant to represent the Kenya Government's system of values' (p. 54). This entails a search for weights which are in keeping with the Kenyan government's objectives. Let A be the weight attached to a £1 benefit accruing to a person with income Y. They assume that A varies continuously as Y changes and then use a host of assumptions, arguments and evidence based on the utterances and actions of the Kenyan government to determine the precise nature of this relationship. While it is a bold effort at evaluating preferences, it is based on a raft of strong and often unrealistic assumptions (e.g. it is assumed that the elasticity of this weight A with respect to income is a constant). The weights derived are interesting to study but it is certainly not advisable to use them for CBA if the choice of projects is very sensitive to these weights.

Since revealed preference models are based on the assumption of governments being rational, a general criticism of using revealed weights in CBA is elegantly summed up by Musgrave's (1969) question, 'If past investment decisions may be assumed to have been correct, why is cost–benefit analysis needed to validate future decisions?'

If one wishes to use governmental value judgements in CBA but at the same time wants to avoid revealed weights, one possible procedure is to present projects as vectors of benefits to the government (i.e. without aggregating the vectors to single numbers representing welfare) and to let the government choose. This method has its difficulties but a discussion of these would go beyond the objectives of the present book.

Another function of revealed weights suggested by Weisbrod (1968) is that they could aid in forecasting government expenditure and its choices among projects. This is clearly an unreasonable expectation; if for no other reason, because weights, as argued in Chapter 2, should be evaluated within localities, and given that an economy changes localities over time, to use yesterday's weights to predict tomorrow's behaviour is likely to be a futile exercise.

Many other uses of revealed preference analysis have been suggested. It is difficult not to feel sceptical about some of them, at least till more sophisticated tools of analysis are developed. At this stage, one major purpose of eliciting governmental weights should be to bring into focus preferences underlying past decisions. Also, revealed preference techniques can be fruitfully used by the decision-maker himself to analyse retrospectively the achievements of projects which have already been implemented and are in progress. He would have to collect information on the *actual* yields of projects and then employ revealed preference analysis to check what preferences of his would have led to this project being chosen. Given that in recent years many large financing groups have begun retrospective evaluation on a regular basis, this use of revealed preference techniques is of considerable practical significance.

The mere act of bringing into focus preferences implicit in past decisions is also more important than may seem at first sight. It helps shape public opinion and ideas about the government and these in turn shape events. A regular analysis of past preferences could act as a scanning device which would put the government on the alert and encourage it to respond by either pointing out errors in the analysis or explaining its decisions. This would hopefully pressurise the government to be more consistent in its future decisions and not to favour groups which do not deserve favour. Instead of judging a government by what it says we could use revealed preference to judge it by what it does – of course, allowing it to criticise our techniques of analysis in turn. A meticulous study of revealed preference is particularly important because comments on government biases and designs based on government plans and budgets are made regularly in newspapers and journals. Even in our everyday conversation we often remark on how a particular decision of the government has more 'sinister' motives. These are all revealed preference judgements. But casual inferences are often erroneous and a formal analysis of revealed preference provides a more erudite basis for commenting on governmental preferences.

Concluding remarks

To castigate a theory or a model emotively serves as little purpose as does passive acceptance of it. In this book an attempt has been made to evaluate some techniques of revealed preference in a scientific manner. In the process of doing this many divergent tools of economic analysis have been used. In places, we have paused to develop some new concepts for analysis. Some of these are of wider interest and could be pursued further. We have refrained from doing so here as it would have been rather tangential to the purpose of this book. However, it may be worth while to indicate some potential lines of enquiry.

While the Weisbrod and UNIDO models have assumed governmental rationality in their analysis of revealed preference such assumptions also underlie large areas of public economics and planning. In this context, we have formally analysed some standard definitions of rationality, many of which are largely behaviouristic. We have argued that rationality often has a non-behaviouristic aspect and moreover that it is not possible, under certain conditions which were discussed in Chapter 4, to demonstrate irrationality purely on the evidence of behaviour.[2] In studying the motivation underlying individual choices, fortunately, the economist does not have to begin from square one. In this area a

---

[2] If rationality was determined purely by behaviour, one would be tempted to modify Aristotle's remark that man is a rational animal to read man cannot but be a rational animal.

vast amount of research has been undertaken by psychologists and one can gain much wisdom from this. Efforts in this direction have already been made (Scitovsky, 1976).

The problem of there being positive evaluation costs has been discussed in the context of governmental decision-making. When a person chooses from alternatives without knowing at all what each will entail, it is like a lucky dip. Evaluation is defined as the process by which this chance element is ruled out. But in most cases evaluation is costly and the question arises as to whether the evaluation itself is worth while or not. This is an important question and deserves attention even outside of revealed preference analysis. A simple model was used here. A more realistic approach would allow for the fact that evaluation could have different degrees and the more one evaluates, the greater the chance of locating the best alternative. This should lead to the analysis of the optimum amount of evaluation.

The concept of quasi-cardinal utility, which has received only cursory attention from psychologists and economists, was treated rigorously here. It is felt that this concept would have significant implications for explaining behaviour under risk. For agents to have definite attitudes towards risk, it is not essential – as is often thought – for utility to be cardinal. For example, a person with a utility scale which is only quasi-cardinal of $1°$, could be a risk-averse person. However, his *extent* of risk aversion is not measurable. This line of analysis was indicated but not pursued in this book.

In the process of analysing interdependence and revealed preference we have examined the logic of the iterated Prisoner's Dilemma. It was demonstrated that the familiar analysis of Luce and Raiffa, which seeks to establish that the sub-optimal equilibrium of the Prisoner's Dilemma will continue to hold even if the game is iterated a finite number of times, is not tenable without a class of rather different and additional assumptions. What happens if these assumptions are not granted? We studied the implications in a simple twice iterated case, but much remains to be done here.

The Prisoner's Dilemma was also used to analyse political constraints. Political constraints severely limit the realm of governmental choice and also affect the nature of its preferences. Hence, no serious attempt to outline practical policies or plans can ignore the importance of political forces.

One of the major concerns of further research should be the use of value parameters in planning. It is argued by most modern economists that an unweighted summation of benefits is an inadequate measure of welfare. The overriding question is whose value weights to use and how to introduce these into planning. Should *revealed* weights be used to calculate the welfare generated by a project, or should projects be left as benefit *vectors* for the government to choose? We offered no firm solution but merely elaborated the difficulties of using *revealed* governmental weights. A more definite answer is necessary to reduce arbitrariness in planning.

A number of analytical results have been established dealing with different aspects of the revealed preference approach, including some theorems on the use of measurability and interpersonal comparability of utility in social evaluation. While the motivation in deriving these has been closely linked with their relevance to the problem of government decisions some of these results are of substantially more general interest.

Many questions have been raised and only some of them answered. It is hoped that to raise a pertinent question is a small advancement towards further knowledge.

Bibliography

Armstrong, W.E. (1939), 'The Determinateness of the Utility Function', *Economic Journal*, vol. 49.

Arrow, K.J. (1951), *Social Choice and Individual Values*, Wiley, New York.

(1959), 'Rational Choice Functions and Orderings', *Economica*, vol. 26.

(1977), 'Extended Sympathy and the Possibility of Social Choice', *American Economic Review*, vol. 67, no. 1.

Banerji, D. (1964), 'Choice and Order: Or First Things First', *Economica*, vol. 31.

Basu, K.C. (1976), 'Retrospective Choice and Merit Goods', *Finanzarchiv*, vol. 34.

(1977) 'Information and Strategy in Iterated Prisoner's Dilemma', *Theory and Decision*, vol. 8.

Blackorby, C. (1975), 'Degrees of Cardinality and Aggregate Partial Orderings', *Econometrica*, vol. 43.

Chase, S.B. (ed.) (1968), *Problems in Public Expenditure Analysis*, Brookings Institution.

Chipman, J.S. et al. (eds.) (1971), *Preferences, Utility and Demand*, Harcourt Brace Jovanovich, Inc.

Datta Chaudhuri, M. and Sen, A.K. (1970), 'Durgapur Fertilizer Project: An Exercise in Economic Evaluation', *Indian Economic Review*, vol. 5.

Debreu, G. (1959), *Theory of Value*, Yale University Press.

Eckstein, O. (1958), *Water Resource Development, The Economics of Project Evaluation*, Harvard University Press.

(1961), 'A Survey of the Theory of Public Expenditure Criteria', in National Bureau of Economic Research, *Public Finance: Needs, Sources and Utilization*, Princeton University Press, reprinted in Houghton (1970).

Fenchel, W. (1953), 'Convex Cones, Sets and Functions', Department of Mathematics, Princeton University (mimeographed).

Fine, B.J. (1974), 'Individual Decisions and Social Choice', PhD Thesis, London University.

(1975), 'A Note on "Interpersonal Comparisons and Partial Comparability"', *Econometrica*, vol. 43.

Fishburn, P.C. (1964), *Decision and Value Theory*, John Wiley and Sons, New York, London and Sydney.

(1970), 'Intransitive Indifference in Preference Theory: A Survey', *Operations Research*, vol. 18.

Freeman, A.M. (1969), 'Income Redistribution and Social Choice: A Pragmatic Approach', *Public Choice*, vol. 7.

Friedman, and Savage, L.J. (1948), 'The Utility Analysis of Choices Involving Risk', *Journal of Political Economy*, vol. 56.

Graaff, J. de V. (1975). 'Cost–Benefit Analysis: A Critical View', *The South African Journal of Economics*, vol. 43.

Hammond, P.J. (1976), 'Equity, Arrow's Conditions, and Rawls' Difference Principle', *Econometrica*, vol. 44.

(1977), 'Dual Interpersonal Comparisons of Utility and the Welfare Economics of Income Distribution', *Journal of Public Economics*, vol. 7.

Harsanyi, J.C. (1955), 'Cardinal Welfare, Individualistic Ethics, and Interpersonal Comparisons of Utility', *Journal of Political Economy*, vol. 63, reprinted in Phelps (1973).

Haveman, R. (1968), Comment on the Weisbrod Model, in Chase (1968).

Heal, G. (1976), 'Do Bad Products Drive Out Good?' *Quarterly Journal of Economics*, vol. 90.

Hicks, J.R. (1939), *Value and Capital*, Clarendon Press, Oxford.

(1956), *A Revision of Demand Theory*, Clarendon Press, Oxford.

Houghton, R.W. (ed.) (1970), *Public Economics*, Penguin.

Kornai, J. (1971), *Anti-equilibrium*, North-Holland.

Kornbluth, J.S.H. (1974), 'Multiple Objective Linear Programming', *Operations Research Quarterly*, vol. 25.

Korner, S. (ed.) (1974), *Practical Reason*, Blackwell, Oxford.

Lancaster, K. (1971), *Consumer Demand: A New Approach*, Columbia University Press.

Layard, R. (ed.) (1972), *Cost–Benefit Analysis*, Penguin.

Lindblom, C.E. (1959), 'The Science of 'Muddling Through' ', *Public Administration Review*, vol. 19.

Little, I.M.D (1950), *A Critique of Welfare Economics*, Clarendon Press, Oxford.

Little, I.M.D. and Mirrlees, J.A. (1974), *Project Appraisal and Planning for Developing Countries*, Heinemann, London.

Luce, R.D. and Raiffa, H. (1957), *Games and Decision*, Wiley, New York.

Lukes, S. (1974), *Power: A Radical View*, Macmillan.

McFadden, D. (1975), 'The Revealed Preference of a Government Bureaucracy: Theory', *The Bell Journal of Economics*, vol. 6. A second part is published in the same journal, vol. 7.

Majumdar, T. (1958), *The Measurement of Utility*, Macmillan.

Marglin, S.A. (1967), *Public Investment Criteria*, George Allen and Unwin Ltd.

Meade, J.E. (1974), 'Preference Orderings and Economic Policy', in Mitra (1974).

Mera, K. (1969), 'Experimental Determination of Relative Marginal Utilities', *Quarterly Journal of Economics*, vol. 83.

Mill, John S. (1848), *Principles of Political Economy*, edited by D. Winch, 1970, Pelican.

Mishan, E.J. (1974), 'Flexibility and Consistency in Project Evaluation', *Economica*, vol. 41.

Mitra, A. (ed.) (1974), *Economic Theory and Planning: Essays in Honour of A.K. Dasgupta*, Oxford University Press, London and New Delhi.

Mukherji, A. (1977), 'The Existence of Choice Functions', *Econometrica*, vol. 45.

Musgrave, R.A. (1969), 'Cost–Benefit Analysis and the Theory of Public Finance', *Journal of Economic Literature*, vol. 7, reprinted in Layard (1972).

Nikaido, H. (1970), *Introduction to Sets and Mappings in Modern Economics*, North-Holland.

Pattanaik, P. (1968) 'Risk, Impersonality and the Social Welfare Function', *Journal of Political Economy*, vol. 76, reprinted in Phelps (1973).

Phelps, E.S. (ed.) (1973), *Economic Justice*, Penguin.

Rapoport, Amnon (1967), 'Optimal Policies for the Prisoner's Dilemma', *Psychological Review*, vol. 74.

Richter, M. (1966), 'Revealed Preference Theory', *Econometrica*, vol. 34.

(1971), 'Rational Choice', in Chipman (1971).

Robbins, L. (1938), 'Interpersonal Comparisons of Utility', *Economic Journal*, vol. 48.

Samuelson, P.A. (1938), 'A Note on the Pure Theory of Consumer's Behaviour', *Economica*, vol. 5. An addendum appeared in the same volume later.

(1955), 'Diagrammatic Exposition of a Theory of Public Expenditure', *Review of Economics and Statistics*, vol. 37, reprinted in Houghton (1970).

(1972), 'Maximum Principle in Analytical Economics', *American Economic Review*, vol. 62, no. 3.

Schick, F. (1977), 'Some Notes on Thinking Ahead', *Social Research*, vol. 44.

Scitovsky, T. (1976), *The Joyless Economy*, Oxford University Press.

Scott, M.F.G., MacArthur, J.D. and Newbery, D.M.G. (1976), *Project Appraisal in Practice*, Heinemann, London.

Sei, F. (1961), 'Political Ceilings on Income Tax', *Public Finance*, vol. 16.

Seigel, S. (1956), 'A Method for Obtaining an Ordered Metric Scale', *Psychometrica*, vol. 21.

Sen, A.K. (1970), *Collective Choice and Social Welfare*, Holden-Day, San Fransisco, and Oliver and Boyd, Edinburgh, 1971.

(1970a), 'Interpersonal Aggregation and Partial Comparability', *Econometrica*, vol. 38.

(1971), 'Choice Functions and Revealed Preference', *Review of Economic Studies*, vol. 38.

(1973), *On Economic Inequality*, Clarendon Press, Oxford.

(1973a), 'Behaviour and the Concept of Preference', *Economica*, vol. 40.

(1977) 'On Weights and Measures: Informational Constraints in Social Welfare Analysis: *Econometrica*, vol. 45.

Shubik, M. (1970), 'Game Theory, Behaviour and the Paradox of the Prisoner's Dilemma: Three Solutions', *Journal of Conflict Resolution*, vol. 14.

Smart J.J.C. and Williams, B. (1973), *Utilitarianism, For and Against*, Cambridge University Press.

Srinivasan, T.N. (1973), 'Tax Evasion: A Model', *Journal of Public Economics*, vol. 2.

Suppes, P. and Winet, M. (1955), 'An Axiomatization of Utility Based on the Notion of Utility Differences', *Management Science*, vol. 1.

Suzumura, K. (1976), 'Rational Choice and Revealed Preference', *Review of Economic Studies*, vol. 43.

UNIDO (1972), *Guidelines for Project Evaluation*, by P. Dasgupta, S.A. Marglin and A.K. Sen; United Nations Industrial Development Organisation, Project Formulation and Evaluation Series, No. 2, United Nations, New York.

von Neumann, J. and Morgenstern, O. (1944), *Theory of Games and Economic Behaviour*, Princeton University Press.

Weisbrod, B.A. (1968), 'Income Redistribution Effects and Benefit–Cost Analysis', in Chase (1968). Reprinted in Layard (1972).

Index of names

Subject index

Agent, economic, defined, 57
Austrian economists, 53

Behaviourism, 53–4, 108
Binary reconstruction property, 35–6, 40, 43
Binary relation, defined, 48
Blocking, 100

Choice function, 48–52
Choice set, 48, 50
Chosen elements, 48, 50
Cone, circular, 37–8, 40, 45
 convex, defined, 36
 convex polyhedral, 13, 45
Cone complement, 37–40, 42–3, 45, 80
Consequentialist ethics, 70
Core, 100
Cost–benefit analysis, 4–5, 63, 72, 92–3, 104–7

Degree of precision, in 2-dimensional analysis, 31–5
 in k-dimensional analysis, 39–40, 42–4, 80
Deontological ethics, 70
Diminishing marginal utility, law of, 68
Distribution of income and welfare, 5, 8, 23, 106

Equity axiom, of Hammond, 65, 70
 of Sen (weak equity axiom), 65, 70
Evaluated choice, 60–2
Evaluation cost and welfare maximisation, 3, 12, 59–64, 109

Feasibility constraints, see Political constraints
Functional combination, defined, 71

G-rationality, 48–51
 potential, 50–1, 54
Gini coefficient, 8
Government, concept of, 6, 44, 57–8
 conflict within, 27, 44–5, 57, 85–6

objectives of, 8, 9, 21–3, 107
Governmental rationality, see Rationality, governmental

Heap paradox, 29
Higher-ordered metric measure, 68

Indifference, concept of, 16, 27–32
Indifference class, defined, 29, 39
Inter-departmental conflict, see Government, conflict within
Interdependence between agents, 4, 84–91, 102–3
Interest-groups, see Lobbies
Interpersonal comparisons, 2–3, 7–8, 27, 65, 68–77, 83
 of differences, 72–3, 83
 of levels, 65, 70, 72–3, 83
 of units, 72–3, 78, 83

Kenya, 106–7

Lausanne approach, 28–9, 42
Learning process, 55
Linear programming, 44
Lobbies, 57, 99–103
Locality, defined, 10

Maximin rule, see social welfare function, Rawlsian
Merit goods, 8–9, 59
Minkowski separation theorem, 25
Motivation, 108
Multiple objective linear programming (MOLP), see Linear programming

Neighbourhood of a ray, 37
Neutral class and zone, defined, 28, 30–1, 39
 with partial comparability, 79–80
Neutrality, concept of, 28

Objective space (O-space), 11–2, 16, 29, 39, 52–3, 55–6, 77, 94, 97–8
Ordering, complete, defined, 72
 quasi-, defined, 52